Till the Moon Be No More

Till the Moon Be No More

The Grit and Grace of Growing Older

Valerie Schultz

A SHEED & WARD BOOK
ROWMAN & LITTLEFIELD
Lanham • Boulder • New York • London

Published by Rowman & Littlefield
An imprint of The Rowman & Littlefield Publishing Group, Inc.
4501 Forbes Boulevard, Suite 200, Lanham, Maryland 20706
www.rowman.com

86-90 Paul Street, London EC2A 4NE

Portions or versions of some of the following work previously appeared in *The Bakersfield
Californian* and *America*.

British Library Cataloguing in Publication Information Available

Library of Congress Cataloging-in-Publication Data
Names: Schultz, Valerie, author.
  Title: Till the moon be no more : the grit and grace of growing older /
    Valerie Schultz.
  Description: Lanham : Rowman & Littlefield Publishing Group, [2024]
  Identifiers: LCCN 2024008083 (print) | LCCN 2024008084 (ebook) | ISBN
    9781538193372 (cloth ; alk. paper) | ISBN 9781538193389 (ebook)
  Subjects: LCSH: Schultz, Valerie. | Aging--Social aspects. |
    Aging--Religious aspects--Christianity. | Christian life.
  Classification: LCC BR1725.S384 A3 2024 (print) | LCC BR1725.S384 (ebook)
    | DDC 248.8/5--dc23/eng/20240511
  LC record available at https://lccn.loc.gov/2024008083
  LC ebook record available at https://lccn.loc.gov/2024008084

For my parents
and my parents' parents
and so on

Contents

CHAPTER 1: Aging in the Generations before Us 1

CHAPTER 2: Lessons of Mortality 13

CHAPTER 3: Incorrect Adages 31

CHAPTER 4: Parallels of Babyhood and Old Age 41

CHAPTER 5: The Politics of Aging. 51

CHAPTER 6: Some Physical and Mental Realities of Aging. . 67

CHAPTER 7: Balancing Outrage and Acceptance 87

CHAPTER 8: In Praise of Invisible Women 101

CHAPTER 9: Circling to Land 111

CHAPTER 10: Generativity and Integrity 119

CHAPTER 11: The Stuff We Leave. 137

CHAPTER 12: The Afterlife 149

Afterword 159

About the Author 161

Aging in the Generations before Us

Do not cast me aside in my old age; as my strength fails, do not forsake me.

—Ps 71:9

When we look back on our lives, our parents and grandparents can seem like they were old before their time. My paternal grandmother acted like she might keel over at any moment, and I later figured out that she was in her forties when I was a kid. Her love of sunbathing had given her the wrinkled, leathery skin of an old apple, and she surrendered to the part. "When you get old . . ." she'd sigh, and leave the sentence unfinished. "This is probably my last trip to see you," she'd say at the beginning of every visit. She lived to be ninety-six or ninety-seven; there was uncertainty about the exact year of her birth. She had designated herself as officially old for fifty years.

Society and the perception of the aging process have changed from the time of our elders, and medical treatments for the ailments of aging have certainly improved, but the fact of aging has not changed.

Every generation thinks they've broken the mold. Maybe it's because the previous generation goes out of their way to tell them all about how things used to be so much better in the old days. My generation of baby boomers believes that we were the first to do everything—that before us, no one ever went to college or got married or gave birth or raised children or took on a mortgage or battled high cholesterol or had a midlife crisis or hit menopause or cared for an aging parent or lost a parent or got laid off or lived in an empty nest. Or retired.

But we actually do retire with more years of life expectancy ahead of us than previous generations enjoyed. We have the privilege of answering the question, What are we going to do with the time we have left?

A not-unrelated question creeps up in unguarded moments: Did I retire too soon?

I did something permanent; I retired from my job in a state prison library just as I turned sixty-one. At the time the decision seemed easy. The year before, we had moved fifty miles away from my job in order to accommodate an excellent promotion for my husband. We agreed that I would only commute for a year, as the drive was exhausting and my salary didn't really justify it. I liked my job, but as a freelance writer, I'd long dreamt of quitting my day job and jumping into writing full-time.

It was a solid plan, and now I've done it. I know I'm lucky by marriage: many of my single coworkers must work further into old age to retire comfortably. I also know that plenty of people not born into the privilege of my circumstances will never be able to retire with any reasonable amount of disposable income, which is a testament not only to the many inequities in our society but to the holes in our tattered social safety nets. If I were single and working my job, I wouldn't even be dreaming about retiring, because my pension would not support me. It now supplements my husband's income (and his future pension). Fortunately, I am covered by his health insurance. I am one-half of a fortunate couple.

But on some days, the thought nags: Did I retire too early? The crossover from work to retirement is proving trickier to navigate than I'd anticipated. Last year, when a coworker died within months of retirement, having fallen ill and been robbed of traveling the world or doing any of the other fun things associated with retirement, I took it as a sign. Then I remembered that signs are only as meaningful as the way you manipulate the data.

I expected a transitional phase. On the first morning after I retired, I felt a little panicky. I thought about all those projects I'd listed, when asked by everyone, that I planned to do in retirement, and I wondered, Do I have to do them all *today*? Can't I just take a day and *lounge*?

I find that I miss the people I worked with for years. I miss our shared catching up, our daily familiarity. Strangely, and in spite of all the annoyances I don't miss, I miss the comfort of the workday routine, of knowing what I'd be doing all day, of feeling that my work matters. Weirdest of all, I miss that Friday feeling: leaving work in delicious anticipation of a glorious weekend of sleep and diversion and not filling in my blocks of hours on a time sheet. Now that every day is Friday, no day recaptures the feeling of Friday.

And I do miss my former paycheck. Although it was smaller than my husband's take-home pay, we feel the loss of my full-time income, especially when we have to weather those calamitous major expenses that happen out of the blue. We are managing our budget, but I am stabbed by guilt when I see my paltry monthly contribution. Did I mess up? Should I have put in more time?

And I face the underlying question: Am I a selfish jerk?

Perhaps it is a question requiring professional help.

People make their own individual decisions regarding retirement, weighing the pros and cons, the benefits and obstacles, the losses and gains. I did that, but I wasn't prepared for these bouts of private second-guessing of my reasons, of my motives, of my trade-offs. I suppose every major life decision dumps its own set of doubts into the psyche.

Going ahead, I want to be worthy of retirement. I don't want to waste any precious free time. I want to make every moment count. Is it possible to fail at retirement? Because I worry that I will, just as I've worried about being a failure at any job I've ever had. "Just don't become a recluse," my husband cautioned. So now I worry about becoming a recluse. But I'm not. I leave the house. I visit my family, my kids, and my sisters. I walk the dog. I do the shopping on weekday mornings, when stores are user-friendly. I spend hours at my desk, rejoicing in words, fretting over words, typing and spilling and welcoming words.

Maybe I am a recluse.

From my retired peers, I've absorbed some rules for retirement: Get enough sleep, but don't get too much sleep. Go outside. Drink lots of water. Answer your phone. Hug more. Use the senior discount. Treasure your health. Do the crossword puzzle. Listen to young people. Live each day like it's your last because one of them is definitely going to be. (This is a tough one: maybe some days are just meant to be throwaways—or not a one, not ever.)

My peers call retirement the new work. They say I will be busier in retirement than I was while working full-time. So far I am not. But I'm new at this. Maybe I will always wrestle with the what-ifs. There are no guarantees that our carefully considered decisions will hold up in hindsight. But it's time to stop whining. It's time to dive into this new chapter without regrets. Each day is a gift and all that. I just need to make peace with myself.

My mother used to tell us kids a lot of stories about her childhood that, when I reflect back on them, make me wish I'd known my grandmother and her sisters, my three great-aunts, when they were young women. Only two of them were mothers, accounting for the ten children among them; the other two were childless their whole lives. When my mother was a kid, her mother and her aunts had been thick as thieves. They communicated—gossiped— over the heads of the children by speaking their own rapid form of pig Latin: it was pig Latin but with extra syllables on the ends of words. It went by too quickly for the kids to decipher. When one of the sisters was being disingenuous or putting on airs, another would say, "Oh, why don't you be yourself!" This may be a common retort in Ireland, but it always sounded deep to me. What a stunningly existential command it is to be told to *be yourself*.

I picture them: young women navigating their way through the privation of the Great Depression (my mother, the fourth of seven, was born in 1931), making do by sharing the several floors of one house and sewing their own clothes and feeding all those kids, all the while being subservient to husbands and the Church's ban on birth control. I would love to ask them about their struggles and triumphs, their joys and sorrows, their scandals and charities. I would love to know if they ever felt they actually did get to *be themselves*. I knew them as old ladies with the kind of ample bosoms that look like they've stuffed a pillow up under their flowered dresses. They had white hair and swollen ankles and false teeth that spent the night in a little ceramic jar on the bathroom counter when they visited, and that my siblings and I would sneak a peek at and then recoil in gratifying horror.

"Consider the generations long past and see," writes the author of Sirach, "has anyone trusted in the Lord and been disappointed? Has anyone persevered in his fear and been forsaken? Has anyone called upon him and been ignored?" (Sir 2:10). To which I answer, "Maybe? How can we know?" I wish I could ask my family matriarchs these questions: Did they, at the end of their lives, feel that, despite their trials and hardships, God's compassion and mercy had followed them all the way home? "Let us fall into the hands of the Lord and not into the hands of mortals," prays Sirach's writer (Sir 2:18), and I join in the prayer that the women who preceded me found themselves in the hands of the Lord.

One of the childless aunts married late in life and then treated her two little dogs like children, getting them groomed excessively and dressing them in dog clothes. She allowed them to sit at the table to eat dinner every night. She threw them birthday parties with hats and favors. My siblings and I thought this was odd and great, since our mother would never have permitted such a guest at our table.

The other childless aunt remained single and independent. She had moved far from home when she was young, from the East Coast to the West Coast, which was unheard of in those days, and had supported herself as a governess. I have since wondered about her sexual orientation, which would never have been discussed back then. She had walked across the brand-new Golden Gate Bridge in San Francisco in the days after they cut the ribbon—not at the same time as the dignitaries and celebrities, she reminded us, but later, with the rabble. After she moved back home to New Jersey, she traveled across the country to visit us on the West Coast even when she was quite elderly, but she took care every time to remind my parents that she had arranged to donate her body to science, so they should call this certain phone number and make sure no embalming took place if she dropped dead at our house. If this gave my parents pause, they never showed it.

My grandmother loved card games and the New York Yankees and the color red and jokes and puns that made her laugh out loud. She outlived two husbands and said a rosary every night only for the first one. She made an amazing four-layer cake by slicing the two layers oh-so-carefully lengthwise in two and then filling the layers in with this pale-chocolate, melt-in-your-mouth homemade frosting. She got her ears pierced when she was ancient, probably in her late sixties, and somehow I was the one deemed the least queasy at shoving the little posts through her hidebound ears. She was thrilled when the nuns at my grammar school taught me to play the guitar for the new folk Masses. She sang along with gusto to "Sons of God" when I practiced the chords at home. You could say my grandmother was an early and ardent supporter of Vatican II.

Some of these stories live in my memory, while some came from my mother's memories. I sometimes wonder what my own children and grandchildren will retain of me and my mother from their own memories and from the stories I've told them. I imagine they'll be as sporadic and unlikely as the ones I've held on to, the ones that would probably horrify my dear old ladies. They died one by one, mostly from cancer, when I was a teenager and then a young mother. But their spirit has lived on in me and now on the page. They were the roots when I was just a branch.

It took Glenn Close to diagnose my ailment.

Here's the main symptom, which my husband and I just had a fight about: since I retired from my job, he finds me irritating. We had a talk (after fighting), and he's right; I am mothering him. Smothering him. Treating him like he is incapable of managing adulthood. "I have a mother," he said. "I want a wife, a partner, a best friend."

It seems I can't stop mothering.

I was an at-home mother during the formative years of my four children's lives. I was also a stealth writer, penciling sentences on the back of the shopping list while waiting for a dance class to end, typing quietly before anyone was awake, and selling essays on parenting to magazines and newspapers for modest fees. But mothering came first. When my kids got older, I worked full-time in a state prison library, where I found that while incarcerated men might seem tough, many of them really needed a mother. As my adult children moved away, my mothering skills were useful in working with hundreds of inmates. I have always been good at mothering.

Apparently, I just don't know when to stop—or whether or not I am supposed to stop.

Thoughts about mothering and not mothering were gnawing at me when I heard Glenn Close's 2019 Golden Globes acceptance speech. She'd just won the Golden Globe for Best Actress for her portrayal of *The Wife*, a woman long obscured by her husband's shadow. "My mom . . . sublimated herself to my father her whole life," Close said. Her words stunned me. That was my mom. That was a whole generation of moms. I often felt sad for my mom for never figuring out who she was beyond her wife and mother roles. But she didn't know how. She didn't know where to begin. The women role models of her childhood and the ensuing decades, when she was sublimating herself to my father and her six children, left her feeling betrayed and abandoned when that long chapter was over. Ever after, she was unhappy, bitter, closed off from life. I loved her, but I never wanted to be her.

I imagine many women listening to that acceptance speech wiped away tears of recognition. Close acknowledged the importance of nurturing our young, but she implored us women to follow our own dreams.

I think of my darlings, now grown-up, and how nurturing them was the most important work I ever did. They long ago fledged from the nest. Now I watch them following their dreams through a precarious and not-always-cooperative world. I am proud of them. Since retiring, however, I have unconsciously slipped into mom mode—more specifically, my mom's mode. I am smothering my kids too. I am hovering. I am worrying. I am feeling unnecessary. I am acting like someone I don't care to be.

Maybe I need to retire from mothering too.

Do mothers retire? I would have said no, that my children would always need some part of me until I die. On an existential level, I know that's true. But while mothering an adult is quite different from mothering a child, the role of mothering is not one that I would have thought we mothers ought to ever relinquish.

This is because we remember. We remember so many intimate things about our children that would embarrass them if we mentioned them today. Like Mary, the mother of Jesus, we can only ponder these things in our hearts. We have known these children since they were in the womb, since they flipped about like fish and made us feel like we were possibly harboring an alien. But we understood in our bones the concept of unconditional love when we gave birth and fell in love in the same instant. We remember inhaling deeply in the folds of our baby's neck. We can still feel the pull of that tiny, astonishingly strong mouth on our breast as clearly as we might remember being slapped really hard. That's a mother's love.

My conflicted thoughts turn again to Mary, a woman with a heart full of these same experiences of mothering. I think of the story in the Gospel of John about a wedding feast she attends with her adult son. "Do whatever he tells you," Mary says to the servants, prodding him to own his mission (Jn 2:1–5). "Woman . . . My hour has not yet come," Jesus tells her in John 2:4, but Mary knows better. Although she walks with her son for the duration of his ministry, even to the foot of the cross on Golgotha, she knows she has already given him over to us. Our spiritual role model for mothering knows when to step in and when to step out of her child's life. Knowing when—and when not—to mother is also a mother's love.

From this I'm learning that my family needs me to let go and follow my dreams rather than sublimate myself to the job my mother never knew how to quit. I suspect that the only person keeping me from embracing personal fulfillment is myself—or the ghost of my mother in me, one woman in a long line of nurturers who didn't know what to do with themselves once their children were grown.

So I'm officially retiring from motherhood—that is, from active motherhood. I will remain in the mother reserves, like the military. You never know, I might be needed. In the meantime my husband can relax. I'm done mothering him. I'll be the one writing the hours away, chasing my dreams, one essay at a time.

As mentioned, we boomers think we are the first generation to experience each stage of life, and that includes aging. We are not, but we do love to document our experiences as though they are brand-new discoveries. We are getting older in great numbers, and that has a historical effect on our country and on our society.

According to the US government's *2020 Profile of Older Americans*, there were 54.1 million people over sixty-five in the United States, comprising 16 percent of the total population. Projections indicate that that percentage will be 21.6 percent by 2040. More than two-fifths (41 percent) of the members of the baby boomer generation are now sixty-five or older.

Old people pose problems for every society. What happens when you can no longer run your own household? What happens when you lose your spouse, or when you have trouble with mobility or cognition or seeing or hearing? What is the obligation of young people to the elderly? We Americans sometimes romanticize the past, waxing poetic about the days when old people were respected, even revered, and lived harmoniously with their married children and grandchildren. We blame industrialization for the memories of old people of meager means crowding into charitable public homes. Today we rely on government programs like Social Security and Medicare to support and protect older citizens. These programs, which are under the continual threat of being cut, often come up short.

The care and treatment of old people varies from society to society and even within societies. When my dad died and my mom became debilitated by Parkinson's, my mom moved into an assisted-living facility. This was possible because she could afford the expensive rent. Otherwise she would have had to live with one of her kids, which would have made everyone involved miserable. She required a level of personal care that we were neither trained nor willing to provide. Increasingly, though, the so-called sandwich generation is tasked with raising children and caring for incapacitated parents in the same house at the same time.

Many of us boomers have wrestled with the problem of caring for aging parents. We know what it's like to have to make difficult decisions about housing and health and money for someone who used to be in charge of us and who perhaps resents our taking charge of them. Now we are the aging parents. How we will age, where we will age, and the grace with which we will cede control of our aging years would be helpful lessons to retain.

I was home from college one summer and found my dad, every night around nine o'clock, microwaving a little bowl of ice cream for our elderly dog. "Twelve seconds," he said. "Then it's not too cold for him." I thought this was old age.

One generation departs and another generation comes, but the world forever stays.

—Eccl 1:4

CHAPTER 2

Lessons of Mortality

The Lord is close to the brokenhearted.

—Ps 34:19

A good friend may have to get rid of her dog—not put him down, I hope and pray, but find him a home where he won't be tempted to bite visitors. My friend has no children, so this dog is like her first child. She adopted him just after she finished grad school and was starting a new life. He has always been protective of her, but lately, he has been growling at random people. Most recently, he took a bite out of her spouse's visiting coworker. The injured party has been gracious about the whole event—the pants are torn, but the wound is superficial—but what if the next time her dog menaces or draws blood from a visitor, they sue her? Worse, what if he bites a child? My friend has taken the dog to obedience training and has been a conscientious dog owner, but it seems like her dog is no longer a good or safe fit for her family.

And her heart is breaking. Her head knows the correct thing to do, but her heart is in pieces.

We grieve for the dead, but sometimes we also grieve for the people or pets who are no longer in our lives. Loss is not always incurred by death. My friend is mourning the potential loss of her companion of eight years. She will do the right thing by her beloved dog; she'll find him a good home and say goodbye if she has to. But man, that leaves a scar.

Grief is an open wound that heals on its own time and never completely. It's liable to split open at the slightest provocation—a snippet of a song, a whiff of something baking, a certain model of car. If it ever completely scars over, you're lucky.

The longer we are alive, the more loved ones we lose. The death of a grandparent is a far different kind of grief than the death of a child, but every shade of grief takes over our hearts. Life is beautiful, and life is painful. Joy and sorrow form us as we age, and they're never in equal proportion.

Parents know that the death of a beloved pet is often a child's first brush with mortality. The death of a goldfish brought about the first time my husband and I, as young parents, were called upon to address the delicate, incomprehensible topic of death. For Christmas our three-year-old had gotten three goldfish, whom she named Cleo, Foxy Wolf, and Multicolor Jake. For a few weeks, the goldfish seemed content in their glass bowl, flitting above the dark blue rocks and the little pirate's chest, overflowing with treasure. They ate their papery-thin flakes of food, and we helped our daughter clean out their bowl according to the directions of the guy at the pet store. But Foxy Wolf started looking lethargic, and her fish scales took on a mushy, unhealthy quality. (Was she female? We had no clue as to fish gender.) We added special drops to the water to kill off any goldfish disease, but it was no use. One morning, Foxy Wolf was belly-up. We put her in a zipper sandwich bag, which my husband took back to the pet store to determine what had gone wrong. He also bought a new fish. But I told my daughter that Daddy had taken Foxy Wolf to the fish vet and that her fish was going to come home good as new.

"Foxy Wolf looks different," said our daughter doubtfully. I looked at my husband in dismay. The markings on the goldfish were off.

"It might be the medicine the fish vet gave her," my husband answered quickly—my husband, the genius. "It might have changed her color a little." This satisfied our daughter. We were such liars. We didn't feel good about it, but we didn't want her little heart to break.

A week later, Multicolor Jake suffered the same fate as Foxy Wolf 1.0, and we knew we could either continue to shield our little one from the reality of death with innumerable replacement fish, or we could honor the demise of Multicolor Jake as a teachable moment. We had to stop lying and tell our daughter the truth about life and death. We had the talk.

The eternal and unfixable absence of some being you love is a hard concept at any age. Our daughter was vaguely aware that living things die, like when Mommy killed a bug in the house or our cat mangled a bird outside. But her face fell and her bottom lip quivered when we told her that Multicolor Jake had gotten sick and died. It was, for my husband and me, the saddest moment of parenthood to date. The demise of a well-loved pet led to the inevitable questions: What if our dog or cat died? What if Mommy or Daddy or her baby sister died? What if she died? We knew it was an important lesson in faith, but we also didn't want to create an obsession with death in her preschool world. We explained that God created us to live our lives here on earth and then to be happy with God forever when we died. I know: this bit of catechism must have sounded pretty alarming to a three-year-old. We assured her that none of us had any plans to go be with God forever anytime soon.

We thought a funeral for Multicolor Jake might help to ease the pain of his loss. Flushing him seemed out of the question.

(Was he male? We had no idea, but his name was, tellingly, Multicolor Jake.) We put his earthly remains in a cardboard jewelry box, which we buried in a shady corner of the yard. We were careful to choose a spot where the dog could not dig him up. We sang a song, said a prayer, and put some rocks in the shape of a cross on Multicolor Jake's grave. We left the picture that our daughter had drawn to commemorate her dead pet. And we moved on. It was the first of many occasions when we were grateful to rely on a tradition to make sense of life. The theology of a fish soul (or, subsequently, of beloved dogs, cats, mice, rabbits, and rats) would come later. For the moment we'd given Multicolor Jake's spirit to God.

You don't have to be a child to mourn the loss of a pet, because you don't outgrow love. We all wrestle with the persistent presence of death in the circle of life. Rituals can give us a sense of control, even though we know control to be an illusion.

Everyone will lose someone—a fact that multiplies the older we get. I lost friends and relatives over the years, but my first dive into the bottomless well of grief came when my father died. I didn't know I could cry that much. I didn't know I could miss someone that much. "Welcome to the club that no one wants to be a member of," a friend said to me soon after my dad died. I'm a double member now that my mom has died. I'm an overgrown orphan.

The experience and episodes of being inconsolable have made me a more compassionate person. The older I get, the more I am aware that, beneath the outward placid faces we may share with the world, everyone is carrying within them unimaginable sadness and heartbreak. No one is immune. I may not know your burdens, but I know how heavy they are. When someone I know is in mourning, I am brought right back there, to the place of my own loss. I sympathize completely. I try to talk less and listen more because I know how compulsively we want to talk about our dead loved ones, how sharing them helps to soothe the soul. One time, after I'd been sobbing in the bathroom weeks after my dad's funeral, my husband, who'd been so kind and supportive throughout my dad's last few months, told me that he was weirdly a little jealous of my anguish. When I didn't understand what he meant, he said he didn't know if he was going to mourn his dad as thoroughly when his time came, because his relationship with his father was less close, more fraught. He felt almost jealous of my grief because it represented the depth of the love I'd shared with my dad. In a way, the deepest grief reflects the greatest joy of having known that beautiful person.

My youngest sister gave birth to her first child a month after our dad died, a daughter who will never know her maternal grandfather, who will only ever hear stories about him. Yet this tiny baby girl testifies to the sacred cycle of life that, even from the bottom of grief, joy can emerge. It's not that the grief gets canceled—far from it. Mourning and rejoicing can happen in the same heart at the same time.

My sister had endured a trouble-plagued pregnancy both physically and emotionally. She did not enjoy being pregnant and couldn't understand why I had liked that time of my life so much. Every time she felt a little better, another complication arose, and I had to admit that if I'd had to jump such hurdles, I would not have retained such rosy memories of pregnancy. My sister wasn't even entirely convinced that she wanted to be a parent. She thought she might like her dogs better than babies. She was afraid that she was going to fail at motherhood.

But the miracle of this baby calmed her fears. Her husband said that the moment their newborn daughter was placed on her mother's chest, he knew that everything was going to be fine. He saw it in her face. Where there was once a couple in love, now there was a family in love.

We who love my sister have been blessed to witness the transformation of a doubter into a mother. My sister is so relaxed and confident around her infant that an onlooker would not know this baby is her first. She has been completely won over. A leery parent has become a loving mother in an instant. My niece herself is a blue-eyed bit of heaven, full of smiles and trills and a sweet baby smell. She is easy to love. A gift from God, she has given our family pure joy and a precious measure of hope.

Passing the old pancake house located down the street from my parents' old house brings me to tears. It isn't the menu that makes me sad but the memories of so many visits to my parents' house when my children were small, when my dad would say, "Who wants some pancakes?" My kids would squeal with delight, and we'd pile into a couple of cars and have a noisy and satisfying breakfast of flapjacks drowning in pools of syrup, Grandpa's treat. My dad would charm the waitress so that his coffee cup was always full, and my kids would fight over who got to pour the cream from the little tin pitcher into his coffee.

I can't remember the last time I had pancakes there; my dad has been dead for years, and my children are grown. But as I drove by, I pictured us in the parking lot—all hair ribbons and missing teeth and pure joy in the day, and I cried. This neighborhood often reminds me of a Frank Sinatra song I'd heard on the record player when I was a kid, the one about seeing a loved one in all the old familiar places and missing them terribly.

I don't cry much anymore about the loss of my dad, but as I cruise the old neighborhood, I'm remembering a day several years after he died, when I felt especially fragile after a two-day visit with my mother. My mother suffered from advanced Parkinson's disease, which was bad enough, but her doctor had begun to use the "A word": Alzheimer's. My siblings and I had attributed her increasing dementia to the Parkinson's, but she somehow seemed worse with the new label. Not much was familiar to my mother in those days, especially since she lived in a retirement facility with a full-time caregiver instead of in the old familiar places. At one point she thought my dad was at the door. "I want to go back," she said to me. "I don't know how I got here." I explained for what felt like the thousandth time about the Parkinson's and the broken hip and her many physical incapabilities, but she waved me away, impatient with facts she didn't recognize as pertaining to her. She wanted me to take her home, but her home had been sold. "I fell while I was Christmas shopping," she insisted. This wasn't true. "Okay," I said. What else could I do but stop talking and let her create her own history? How I used to fret about how to make my mother happy, even though I knew I couldn't make her happy.

Still, sometimes I want to go back too. We'd all like to cheat time's passage—we try all sorts of trickery—but all we have is today. This blessed day. My folks are gone; my husband and I say, "What did you say?" to each other a lot; and my children are adults—and this is all exactly as it should be. Still, a visit to the past often turns unfinished and unsettling.

I pass the pancake house on my way to the cemetery before I head home. It's Halloween, and I want to make the two-hour drive home before the trick-or-treaters come calling. I bring a little bunch of orange marigolds and tidy up around my folks' grave markers. A funeral is in progress just over the next rise of the cemetery; there's a hearse and a canopy and lots of people dressed in black. We all have our beloved dead. Their photos take center stage on our Día de los Muertos altars. More faces are added each year. The melancholy Sinatra song persists in my head. I blow my nose, get on the freeway, and drive away from all the old familiar places.

I used to try find the words to bring peace and acceptance to my mother's agitated heart. But I couldn't. My attempts only distressed her. "I try to make deals with God," she told me in a lucid moment. "But he isn't having it." This is the deal: God is with us, but God doesn't send us back to the way things were. We only make our way ever closer to our rest in the divine.

✦

When I visit my dad now, he is under a stone. Or, that is, his ashes are, with his anchor set in the older part of the cemetery under a big old oak tree. It's peaceful. We buried him in the month of July, when the tree's shade cooled his resting place. The ever-progressing seasons strip away the leaves, deposit acorns everywhere, leave my dad under bare branches with no shade, and then gradually replenish the green bower. I write this in the brief space between the end of winter and the beginning of full-on spring. The tiny new leaves and the tilt of the earth leave my dad's marker just outside the reach of shade, which is fine. My dad loved, even worshipped, the sun.

I say hello to the neighbor to my right (his left): a fellow named Pierce, who's been here since 1967, an old-timer. My dad moved into the area in 2009. Pierce is old enough to be my dad's father. Pierce's wife, Phyllis, who resides next to him, was born one year before Pierce and subsequently died one year before him. They both died at the age of fifty-one. I wonder what cut their lives short. I also wonder if their lives were always that eerily in sync.

On my dad's other side rests Raymond, who arrived in 1981 or perhaps 1989—the final raised-up number of his date of death is broken. Raymond's wife Helen moved in just before my dad, in 2008. Raymond's stone has symbols on it that I don't get, secrets I'm not in on. My dad's plaque notes his U.S. Navy service, QMS2. Pierce's marker is engraved with flowers, matching Phyllis's exactly.

There are rituals I perform when I visit my dad. I start by trying to remember the most direct route to his grave through the cemetery's winding maze of narrow paved roads. I do this unconsciously, having been taught by my dad that it's almost criminal not to take the shortest route to any given destination. He chafed at having to go anywhere he deemed out of his way. I play my dad's kind of music in the car: Tony Bennett or Gene Kelly smoothly singing. If they're in season, I bring homegrown roses. I wrap the stems of the roses in wet paper towels covered with foil, just like he taught me. My dad grew roses everywhere he lived and always used to send me home with a bouquet of his roses, wrapped just this way for a safe journey. The roses will go in the vase that is embedded just below my dad's marker. Pulling the inverted vase up out of the ground takes more strength than I think I have, but once it is extricated from the muck of bad weather, I turn it right side up and fill it with water from the spigot. The roses safely in the vase, I use the wet paper towels to clean the dust and pine needles and dead leaves off his marker.

I bring a small stone and leave it on the edge of the marker. I think the stones get mowed awry by the caretakers after I leave, so I hunt around Raymond, Helen, Pierce, and Phyllis to retrieve stones from past visits. Today I find four. I line them up and add a fifth. I believe this is a Jewish custom, which we are not, and whenever I do this, I resolve to google the meaning of leaving a stone or pebble at a grave. Then I forget.

When my tidying chores are done, I talk a little to my dad, as well as to God. I live a hundred miles from this patch of green, so my visits are sporadic. I like to come here whenever I'm in the neighborhood, which isn't as often as I'd like. Sometimes I cry. Sometimes I don't. Today a woman offers me a pamphlet on the topic of *Losing a Loved One*. It has her church's strings attached. I refuse it gently. "Save paper," I say.

Some people don't like cemeteries and never return there after the funeral. Cemeteries give them the creeps, or they prefer to remember their loved one alive. I understand that. Cemeteries aren't for everyone. I find these visits peaceful, a pause in a hectic life. The time I spend here recharges my love for the living and the dead, and it rekindles my resolution to try to live in a way that would make my dad proud.

Soon the shade of summer will again shelter my dad, and the caretakers will hammer into the ground the signs warning of rattlesnakes, and the number of dead in the cemetery will increase. As I leave, a pack of motorcycles weaves slowly into the cemetery, their engines growling softly, ridden by mourners whose visits are just beginning. I nod to them, "Sorry for your loss. See you next time."

To be Catholic is to make your peace with mystery. It is a matter of faith that some of the things Catholics believe in, like the Trinity or the virgin birth or the transubstantiation of bread and wine into Jesus's body and blood, cannot be explained. The human rational mind cannot fathom the mind of God. "Where were you when I founded the earth?" God demands of the presumptuous human Job (Jb 38:4), and we Catholics must make our peace with that.

I say, "make peace with mystery," but barring that, we are at least well acquainted with mystery. At a young age, we memorize the Mysteries of the rosary—five each of the Joyful, Luminous, Sorrowful, and Glorious—which represent key occasions in the lives of Jesus and his mother, Mary. When we pray a rosary, we contemplate just one set of five Mysteries, depending on what day it is. This sounds more complicated than it is in practice, especially if you have grown up saying the rosary.

The Mysteries of the rosary help to remind us of the tenets of our faith. I am thinking specifically today of the Sorrowful Mysteries, which are, in order, the agony in the garden, the scourging at the pillar, the crowning with thorns, the carrying of the cross, and the crucifixion. These illustrate the story of the final days of Jesus's earthly life, including how the Romans tortured and executed him as a criminal. The Gospels tell us that these events immediately preceded Jesus's resurrection, the Glorious Mystery that is the main deal with the Catholic creed.

Sometimes I try to imagine what it must have been like for Mary to accompany her son throughout those last awful moments of his life, how her heart must have burst with grief at losing him. But I think anyone who has ever lost a loved one, no matter the circumstances, knows that grief intimately. We mourn those who have died, and then we go on with our lives, but we hold that hard stone of grief in our hearts. It never leaves us.

My mother once explained to me that she'd been named for the Sorrowful Mysteries: the Dolors (sorrows) of Mary became Dolores Marie, her baptized name. "What a heavy lift for a little girl," I thought. It occurred to me that perhaps my mother's name had either prompted or encapsulated her innate negativity. She never failed to note a downside. My mother never stopped hating her name. She wanted be known as Dee even to her grandchildren. She once told me that her father had wanted to name her Dagmar, an exotic might-have-been that still made my mom feel wistful, but he'd been voted down. Her father died when my mother was two, and I think the grief of losing him colored her whole life, even if she barely remembered his death. She mostly remembered his absence: the man who loved her best simply wasn't there anymore. It was her first and greatest and most lasting sorrow.

And maybe each of us has our own set of Sorrowful Mysteries. If we tried, we could probably list our particular Sorrowful Mysteries in chronological order. We may have more or fewer than five, but these are the crosses we have carried, the thorns of sadness that have pierced us on our journey. Our own Sorrowful Mysteries give us sharp insight into the actual *sorrow* of the Sorrowful Mysteries of the rosary, making the suffering and death of

Jesus resonate in our soul. We identify with the Sorrowful Mysteries because we have experienced our own.

The recent anniversary of my father's death has prompted these thoughts on how the pang of loss never leaves us no matter how much time elapses and no matter how much life we have lived in the meantime. During the years when we mourn someone, we also mark our own Joyful or Luminous or Glorious Mysteries, our delights and wonders and milestones, but the sorrowful ones lurk deep down in our beings, bonding to our emotional DNA.

Our Mysteries are personal, but they give us an understanding of the universal. We share human traits with all other humans, a fact we forget with too much ease. But our shared humanity is perhaps the reason we can come together in times of local or national or global tragedy: we may be separated by distance or race or creed, but we know exactly what it feels like to lose, to suffer, to mourn—just as we know how to help, to console, to love.

The Sorrowful Mysteries, which Jesus endured while incarnated as a man, can comfort us in a time of loss because we know that God does not leave us to grieve alone. God will never desert us because God, although divine and perfect and all-knowing, has been there. How's that for a mystery?

As I get older, the hazy memories I have of my early childhood are no longer checkable. Since my folks are gone and my siblings are younger, I have no one to corroborate the truth of whether something had happened or I'd only imagined it. Did our mean neighbor really throw our swing set into the pond? Did we ever even live near a pond? Were the walls of my bedroom really charcoal gray? The few photos I have of the times that predate my conscious memory are black and white, so some of these things are forever unknown.

And I wonder sometimes if a memory is genuine or if the extant photo just makes me think I remember. I'm not sure if I really remember being the four-year-old girl in the family photo, the one with all of us wearing our Sunday best, with my tired-eyed mother holding the new baby and my older brother looking picture-perfect and me in my checkered dress with the crinoline, where I'm holding my father's hand and sticking out my tongue, probably ruining the photo session. Do I remember the feel of my father's sturdy hand? Or have I just seen the photo enough times to place myself there?

The same feeling of helplessness takes hold of me when I read through my parents' old letters and they mention a name with which I am unfamiliar, a friend or classmate or navy buddy. Who would know who this person was? Who would remember? Then I realize that anyone I could ask is gone. I wish I'd read their letters and asked them detailed questions when they were alive, when the letters sat in a cardboard barrel in the garage, although reading your parents' private letters when they're still alive may be one of the more intrusive things a kid can do.

Our histories are important to us, but they do not outlive us. There are things about my parents I will never know, even as their lives are immortalized in old letters. Our personal past forms us, but it does not outlast us. It may not even last as long as we do, as is witnessed by my inability to answer my own questions: Did we have that silly beagle when we lived in that town? What was the name of that old neighbor? Who was the guy who dressed up like Santa but smelled like old whiskey when he ho ho hoed?

My oldest living uncle is writing down his memories for posterity through some online program that gives him prompts, and he calls me sometimes with a random question, usually about my folks. Sometimes I'm able to help him out, but not always. His most recent attempted foray into my memory was his asking, "What was the name of that bar down the street where your dad and I got to feeling good sometimes?" It escaped me. I told him

I remembered the bar because I remember sneaking into the bar through the back door with the owner's son for some underage drinking and making out, but my uncle didn't want to know about that. Neither of us could remember the name of the place. My younger cousin found it online in a matter of moments.

We picked up Ringo's ashes today.

Our dog Ringo might have been seventeen, eighteen, or even nineteen. We don't know, because he came to us past puppyhood. He was rescued from the streets of Hollywood by our daughter and her friend, who'd named him Ringo Starr. Then they discovered that their apartment management wouldn't allow them to have a dog, which is how Ringo arrived at our house and made his way into our hearts. He was a timid fellow who had to learn not to eat out of the trash, to trust that we would actually give him a bowl of dog food twice a day. Male voices scared him. He wouldn't come near my husband for several weeks.

Ringo never got the hang of playing with dog toys; in fact, he'd bark at other dogs chasing a ball or being otherwise frisky. This earned him the nickname the Fun Police. Small children made him nervous, like there was something not right about some little human looking at him eye to eye. But he turned out to be an excellent watchdog. No one approached our house without him alerting us, at least until his hearing and eyesight went bad.

Life moves to a schedule when you have a dog; there's walk times and feeding times and the location of the sunny spot throughout the day. You get used to the rhythm of your dog's needs. You arrange your own appointments and travels around your dog's timetable. You don't want to leave him alone too long in the house or out in the yard too long after dark. You clean up after him when he eats too much grass, and you comfort him when thunder makes him tremble. You may even buy him a raincoat, which he will hate wearing.

When your dog dies, there are empty spaces in your day and in your heart.

We are sad to be dogless, even though it makes some things easier for us. We don't have to walk anyone in the rain or late at night. We don't have to hire a dog sitter anytime we go away overnight. We won't pay the vet bills an elderly dog incurs. But these are thoughts for another day. Today we just miss our very good boy. We miss his face at the door when we get home; even when he was old and infirm, Ringo still greeted us with unconditional love. We miss his insatiable desire for treats. We miss having to carry him up and down stairs. We miss the sound of his breathing in the wee hours. We will cry a little the next time we have pizza and no one begs for a crust.

Ringo was returned to us today in a little velvet bag with an embroidered saying: "Until we meet again at the Rainbow Bridge." He weighs hardly anything. Our vet's office sends us a sympathy card with Ringo's paw print enclosed, printed by a kind vet tech after his death. I think of all the dogs that may be waiting for us at the Rainbow Bridge, not to mention the cats and rabbits and fish and mice. It may be a crowded reunion.

I plan to bury Ringo's ashes under a rosemary plant. The resident deer that regularly eat my flowers don't like rosemary because of its strong fragrance. I could opt for lavender or mint, which are also deer resistant. But I'm picking rosemary, with a nod to dear old Shakespeare, for remembrance.

We'll remember.

One day I suddenly remembered the chant I learned in childhood: "Ladybug, ladybug, fly away home! Your house is on fire and your children will burn!" It struck me as an excessively cruel little song. Did my mother teach me this? I'm hoping I didn't teach it to my children. When I saw it in print in an old book of nursery rhymes at a used-book sale, I decided not to buy it for my granddaughter.

We parents worry that our children will burn literally and metaphorically. Our hearts can hardly bear it when a parent loses a child, any child, let alone a child we also knew and loved. Any family that loses a young person knows the sound and the feeling of their hearts cracking in two. The passing of time is meaningless to the whole family's grief. There will always be a terrible hole in the fabric of the family. I speak from tragic experience.

We parents shoulder the responsibility for our children's well-being when they are babies and as they grow up, but the time comes when we have to let them fly away from our home. We can't save them from a burning house that is not our house. We give them life and then we have to give them their lives, trusting God, the universe, the angels, and the fates to guard and keep them.

The ashes that mark our foreheads on Ash Wednesday only last for a day, but the ashes on our hearts are meant to endure for the entire forty days of Lent. The ashes are drawn on us as a sign of repentance, of our yearning for God's forgiveness, of our intent to live our faith more truly in the face of our mortality.

The black cross of ashes is especially real when one is mindful of the death of a loved one, as I was this year, when Ash Wednesday coincided with the first anniversary of my mother's death. The mother I'd known had really departed a few years before her physical death; by the time she'd died, she was not herself. She was rarely cognizant of anyone or anything. As I walked forward this year to receive the ashes on my forehead, I suddenly remembered another Ash Wednesday a few years ago. On that day, my mother was still able to get around with some help, and she called my younger sister on the phone, insisting that she be taken to church to get her ashes. Although we aren't supposed to speak ill of the dead, I will say my mother was a difficult woman who was devout only when it suited her. She had neither gotten ashes nor attended Mass in years. I reminded my poor sister, who was in the middle of a busy day with young children, that this was another of our mother's attempted manipulations to get one of us to drop everything and do her bidding. This was, after all, the same woman who sat in her gentleman friend's car every Sunday outside the church while her caregiver attended Mass.

Neither one of us had taken her for ashes that year.

So as I received the ashes on my forehead this year as a sign of repentance and as the priest intoned, "Remember, you are dust and to dust you shall return," I understood my great need for forgiveness. Because even in my memories, I was guilty of ignoring my mother's demands and of judging her intentions.

On this Ash Wednesday, I had taken off work in order to spend the day with my younger sister. We were going to the cemetery later to remember our mother together and to put flowers on her grave. I went for ashes in the old neighborhood, at the parish of my teenage years, where my younger siblings had made their First Communion and where my folks had renewed their wedding vows on their fiftieth anniversary. After Mass I passed my old high school and the exact spot on the street where I'd gotten my first parking ticket. I passed Earl's Donuts, where the hot ones came out of the oven around two in the morning, and our old street—gated, so I was no longer permitted to drive through—where my family had lived and I'd thought my parents were ancient when they were in their forties.

Ashes on my forehead as a sign of repentance.

My grief at my dad's death seven years ago was guilt-free. I'd loved him to his last second and done everything I could for his care. My dad lived his life with joy, and I miss him fiercely and purely. My grief at my mother's passing, in contrast, elicits a mix of guilt, regret, confusion, and confession for all the times I wished she would finally get it, would acknowledge and be grateful for her many blessings, would accept herself and us as we were, would love us back without condition.

Ashes on my forehead as a sign of repentance.

Losing a parent is hard, and mourning a parent with whom you know you could have been more patient and loving when she was alive is harder still. My mother was sick for a long time, and she was not saintly about suffering. I was often irritated with her behavior. I wanted her to be someone else. I understand now that it was my job to accept her just as she was, and I didn't. I wore the ashes this year with an awareness of my shortcomings as a daughter, a pain that sits on my heart now in the form of ashes. Lent is for starting over, but some things can't be redone. I can only pray that repentance brings forgiveness from the God who loves us hugely in spite of our sins.

By the rivers of Babylon, there we sat and wept, remembering Zion.

—Ps 137:1

CHAPTER 3

Incorrect Adages

The glory of the young is their strength, and the dignity of the
old is gray hair.

—Prv 20:29

When I turned fifty, a lot of other people were turning fifty—other
boomers. I saw so many magazine covers proclaiming some version of "Fifty is the new thirty!" You know what? It isn't. Although
we'd love it to be so, fifty is not the new thirty. Thirty-year-olds
have been aging into fifty-year-olds for centuries, and that fact has
not changed. Some people look fantastic at fifty, and some people
look like hell. Some people feel fantastic at fifty, and some people
feel like hell. Some people don't make it to fifty. Or thirty. What
I'm saying is the silly slogans we old people parrot are not helpful.

This applies to the reliably useless assertion "You're as young
as you feel." I know this adage is well-intentioned, but you're not.
You are the age the calendar verifies. You may be more or less
debilitated than a person born the same day as you, but the state
of your health doesn't make you objectively younger or older, and
neither do your feelings. Numbers don't lie. The body and mind do
not lie. I do, however, recommend keeping an open mind, which

may help you act a little younger than your years. A closed mind will age you faster than your climbing blood pressure. An attitude of curiosity will also help you understand and navigate the changing world a little better.

When a young person opens the door for you, you do not have to say, "Age before beauty!" They've heard this from every old person before you. It's clear that age and beauty can coexist. Also, everyone is aging every day, just at different rates and in different ways. Also, everyone's ideal of beauty may differ from yours. Deal with it.

When you watch the network news, which you only do with any regularity if you are old, you do not have to say, "The world is going to hell in a handbasket!" First of all, what is a handbasket? Who uses such a thing anymore? Do you carry stuff around in an antiquated basket with a handle? And why would a handbasket be on its way to hell anyway? Second of all, the world has never been a perfect place—not ever, not for anyone. The Middle Ages had the Black Plague, and the seventies had hip-huggers. Third of all, clichés and platitudes are for the lazy.

The statement "Youth is wasted on the young" is fraught with a frivolous regret that has no relevance to the young person in question. And how do you think that makes the young person you're talking to feel? Are you insinuating they're wasting the early years of their adult life? They're not, and that's rude. There may be things you're sorry you didn't do when you were young. You may rue the time you think you wasted in your youth. But your issues are not the young person's problem. You're not dead yet, so get going, and do whatever it is you wish you'd done (within reason). Say it with me: "Youth is not wasted on the young." Youth is just the state of being young.

The old chestnuts we slip into conversation at every opportunity are irritating. It's like old folks have a script to follow. We don't have to fit in a truism every time we speak. My paternal grandmother, God rest her soul, was visiting my uncle, her son, in a nursing home. He was not well; in fact, he was dying from emphysema. "Well," my grandmother said as part of her schtick, "I always say, when you have your health, you have everything." Really, Grandma? That's the pleasantry you came up with here? You realize you're saying, in effect, that your son effectively now has nothing? That's not exactly comforting.

I used to be irritated by what I thought of as my mother's autopilot. When some topic of conversation triggered a (somewhat) related story in my mother's brain, she had to tell it—*had to*. She could not be deterred. She had to tell the whole thing from beginning to end every time, like the hundredth performance of a memorized one-act play. Any interruption, like mentioning that she'd already told you this story, hahaha, was either ignored or, worse, sent my mother back to the beginning of the loop. She couldn't *not* say her preprogrammed piece. I have since noticed this foible in other old people and, God forbid, in myself. My daughter's story about some inconvenience of early motherhood, for example, doesn't need my instant follow-up of some story from her babyhood that she's already heard—several times. When I sense the autopilot engaging, I disengage it. I swallow the words before they can begin their journey out of my mouth, thinking, "Cut the power to the engines!" I fear there will come a time when, like my mother, I no longer know where the off switch is.

On the other hand, I appreciate the snappy sayings we like to share about aging, like "It beats the alternative!" or "It's not for the faint of heart!" or "That's a senior moment!" But these lighthearted observations only resonate with other aging people. They offer the kind of humor where you really have to be there, at that later stage of life, to get it. We seniors know that old age is not for wimps, that our daily aches and lapses are crosses we bear without fanfare, and that we are not alone in our secret slips and fears.

"Don't get old," my mother used to tell me, and I think she was serious. She didn't want to hear the thing about getting old beating the alternative, which was death. She just wanted to turn back the clock and stay young, by which I mean she wanted to stay relevant. She wanted to be in the thick of things. My mother was the original poster girl for FOMO, the fear of missing out. She wasn't interested in aging gracefully or surrendering focus to the next generation. I don't know if she was ever truly happy again after she turned fifty, which turned out not to be the new thirty.

❖

I'm remembering a news item I saw a few years back about a sort of modern-day Wolfman. An overly hairy man who performed daredevil stunts in a Mexican circus, he exhibited a phenomenon known as hypertrichosis. As arresting as this fellow was, it was the spin that maybe this guy's genes held the cure for baldness that really caught my attention: the *cure* for *baldness?* Was baldness now considered a disease like polio, an illness like malaria? If I were a bald man, I would have written a strongly worded letter. But I am only married to a bald man.

I imagine the proud bald men of the Washington, DC–based organization Bald R Us would respond vehemently to the idea of baldness as an affliction to be eradicated. Their bumper stickers state their opinions clearly: "God created a few perfect heads, and on the rest, he put hair," says one. "I'm too sexy for my hair," asserts another. "Just say, 'No!' to rugs and plugs," advises a third, referring to toupees and hair-transplant surgery. They believe that bald is beautiful. Their mascot is—yes—the bald eagle.

My smooth-headed, beautiful husband developed a theory explaining why men sometimes go bald at a young age, as he did, saying it goes back to the time of cavemen, when the women had to choose carefully from among the horde of potential mates. Savvy women were able to pick out the men who would be virile fathers and good providers, as well as intelligent and good-humored partners, by looking for the bald heads—like my husband's.

His folklore is fascinating but faulty: baldness is actually caused by a combination of factors, such as hormonal changes (including high testosterone) and family history, not to mention aging. Baldness, the scientific name for which is alopecia, can be temporary or permanent. It affects both men and women, although men overwhelmingly own the receding hairlines.

In spite of the snappy bumper stickers, the unfortunate reality is that premature baldness is considered neither beautiful nor desirable in our appearance-obsessed society. While women have many physical features over which to fret—hair, eyebrows, eyelashes, nose, lips, neck, upper arms, hands, bust, waist, derriere, thighs, calves, ankles, feet, and perhaps a few more that I've missed—men are mainly judged on hair and height. Height is a tough attribute to enhance, but hair is doable. Hair is to be kept at all costs, and the price of restoring hair—or the illusion of hair—can be exorbitant. Men who start to go bald resort to drastic measures, toupees and tonics and drugs and weavings and painstaking hair implants, to arrest the upward creep of the hairline. Male movie stars are especially sensitive to baldness because, once an actor is bald, he may not be as likely to be cast as the leading man. His roles may decrease to the male lead's best friend or the bumbling neighbor/bureaucrat/evil henchman—who is bald.

Hats, a cheap alternative to the expensive false-hair industry, are the friend of the bald man. It can be a shock when a bald man takes off his hat for the first time because we tend to assume that hats cover hair. But hats are a very practical accessory for the naked head. My husband has an array of hats that keep his head warm in the winter and unsunburned in the summer. His favorite souvenir to buy wherever we travel is a baseball cap. And he never has to worry about hat hair.

"Grass doesn't grow on a busy street," my maternal grandfather used to say, trumpeting the superior brainpower sheltered by his bald head. His intelligence was but one attribute to flaunt: my grandfather would be glad—or perhaps embarrassed—to know

that, according to a survey cited by the boys of Bald R Us (www
.baldrus.com), a sampling of wives of bald men consistently rated
the romantic abilities of their husbands a 7 or higher on a scale of
1 to 10, while the wives of men with full heads of hair gave their
husbands a score of 5 or less. Maybe they'll add "Bald men do it
better" to the bumper sticker collection.

Mother Nature's little joke is that, as a bald man ages, he
often grows hair in unsightly places: the ears or the nose or the
shoulders, on every surface except the one upon which he would
prefer to grow hair, which is the top of the head. Many bald men
I know grow mustaches and beards and goatees, perhaps because
they can. Facial hair provides a visual contrast to a bald head and
a comforting thatch to stroke when its owner is deep in thought.

The interesting conundrum for my husband has been that,
when he was younger, his hairline made people think he was older,
but now that he is older and bald, people think he is younger.
They are surprised by his age. This may be because it has become
stylish for younger men who are balding to go ahead and shave
their whole heads as though they're affirming that baldness was
really their idea all along. I think this proud, polished look is an
improvement over the days when men grew whatever hair they
could grow superlong in order to wrap the sorry strands about
the balding spots in the misguided look known as the comb-over.
Young bald men are changing society's perception of baldness
one shining head at a time. When popular athletes and entertainment figures are bald, they affirm that they certainly don't need
to be *cured* of anything. They help bald men everywhere to hold
their lovely heads high. As the saying goes, they're too sexy for
their hair.

Time is a construct, and time is on our side and all that, but
here's the kind of online observation about time that can blow

your mind: 1970 and 2022 are as far apart as 1970 and 1918. This proves that time is definitely moving faster than it did when I was a kid.

Even as we attempt to give a rest to the use of incorrect sayings about age, and even as we want to keep up with the young people, I advise caution in adopting their lingo. Years ago my teenagers drew a line in the sand and told me in no uncertain terms that I was not to say ever again that I was "down with" something. I thought I was being cool. I was not. They insisted that moms just don't talk like that, even though I heard them say it all the time.

Nevertheless, with my kids grown and gone, I find myself parroting some of the things I hear young people say as I go about my business. I am like an archaeologist who has found some captivating runes. For example, I've noticed that people under thirty—rather than saying, "You're welcome" after I've said, "Thank you" for something—usually reply, "Of course." Of course? Do they mean that of course there is no argument that they would always have done whatever it is I'm thanking them for? Or that of course I am welcome, so why am I even saying, "Thank you"? I don't know how or when that started, but it seems to be the standard reply now. The last time someone thanked me for holding a door, I couldn't help myself. "Of course," I said. Of course I would hold the door for you, old person.

When I enter a retail business these days, the young person working the front of the store invariably says, "Welcome in!" What's with the addition of the word "in"? Using just plain "Welcome" seems like an all-encompassing word of greeting. Where else would they be welcoming me into? It surprises and then educates me that new words and phrases and lingo are added to our verbal communications all the time. One of my children uses the pronouns they/them, and when I mentioned that it seemed difficult to remember to use what I think of as plural words to refer to a singular person, their partner gently chided me that, as a writer, I should be especially cognizant that language is a living, organic, changing thing. They were right. I stand corrected. I welcome them in.

My young niece recently asked me what I'd worn to my "ho-co." It took me a minute to contextualize this shorthand: her mom had sent me a photo from my niece's first homecoming dance. Ah! "Ho-co" meant homecoming. I'm fascinated by the shortening of words as though time is too short to enunciate the whole term. I resisted saying that she looked "adorbs." Especially riveting are the abbreviations of words, initially used in text messaging, that people now say aloud in conversation. (That same niece recently texted me "ofc," which I deciphered as a further tightening of the aforementioned "of course.") Not every acronym makes sense. Saying the letters "BRB" uses the same number of syllables as actually needed to voice the phrase "Be right back," but whatever—or "whatev."

Instead of saying, "I'm sorry" for some wrong done, I've heard young folks say, "My bad." Bad, in my experience, is an adjective, not a noun and not something you can take ownership of, but when you finally give in and find yourself saying "My bad," you find it works just like an apology. It's like you're owning the offense you committed with the understanding that you recognize the value of not doing it again. I like it. But I will probably not be allowed to say it around my kids.

When my daughter and her partner want to emphasize the validity or truth of something, they say, "A hundred percent." Or the stronger version seems to be "100 percent." I find this numerical figure making its way into my vocabulary after I visit them. It's not something I would have ever come up with on my own. I appreciate that they don't resort to 110 percent, a percentage that has always bothered me with its hyperbole: since 100 percent is the whole, the complete total of a thing, let's leave it at that, people.

The other term that has come into common usage, taking the place of agreeing with some premise with the standard "Me, too," is "Same."

As in, you say, "I'm pretty hungry."

Your younger companion says, "Same."

This one I totally get because the #MeToo movement has made that phrase a loaded and powerful confession. Most of us women can respond "Me, too" in any conversation about sexual harassment or assault, statistically over 80 percent of us, according to the National Sexual Violence Resource Center (www.nsvrc.org), so using a more benign word to signify a point of less weighty agreement is less triggering. I try to use "Same" all the time now, even though I am not a young person, because I do number myself among that 80 percent of us. I am hopeful that, thanks to the #MeToo movement, far fewer younger women will experience sexual harassment or assault in the workplace or the church or the home or the school or the street or anywhere else. If we can name it and expose it, perhaps we can curtail it.

Even till I am old and gray-headed, do not forsake me, O God.

—Ps 71:18

CHAPTER 4

Parallels of Babyhood and Old Age

More and more, humble your pride; what awaits mortals is
worms.

—Sir 7:17

"The world," wrote Ralph Waldo Emerson, "when seen through a
little child's eyes, greatly resembles paradise." My eyes have never
been good. I got fitted for my first pair of glasses for nearsight-
edness in the fourth grade, which was revelatory: the world was
so *crisp*. The trees across the street had distinguishable, individual
leaves. The bank building had a clock with moving hands. Did
normal people see like this all the time? I was amazed by my
corrected eyesight.

I tried not to wear my glasses through much of high school,
whipping them out only to see the board in class or to watch a
movie once the theater went dark. I was a book nerd, but I didn't
want to look like one. My vanity led my fellow students to think
I was a snob since I never waved back to them when they waved,
but it was because I couldn't see them. I had to rely on my glasses
to drive a car; it said so on my license because I couldn't have
passed the DMV eye test without my glasses in a million years. I

graduated to contact lenses in college. I had to add reading glasses in middle age. Now I wear bifocals and have been told that cataract surgery is in my future. Weirdly, a result of that surgery may be that I will no longer need glasses. That feels like a full circle.

But I am no longer that fourth grader, so looking at the world through the eyes of a child does not come easily to me. Jesus tells us to become like little children if we want to follow him to the kingdom of heaven (Mt 18:3), but I am ridiculously far from childhood. And as I approach old age, I don't want to become literally like a child. I actively fear the return of childlike dependence on someone for my physical care—specifically, the intimate kind of caring I did for my dad and mom. I want to remain self-sufficient, considering the world through the eyes of an independent adult. How good of God, then, to make me a grandma so that I can't help but observe life's journey through a beloved child's eyes.

From the moment of her birth, my granddaughter has retaught me one of the gifts of the Holy Spirit that we learn at confirmation: a sense of wonder and awe. As adults, we feel those big feelings mostly when we encounter big things: the Pacific Ocean, the Grand Canyon, the mighty forces of nature's storms, the photos from the moon. But when you spend the day with a child, you note anew the fascinating aspects of small things. I watch my eleven-month-old granddaughter give her total focus to picking up a squashed raspberry with pincerlike fingers or finding the tag on a fuzzy stuffed lamb. She is not in a rush. And neither am I. She smiles broadly every time she sneezes—every time. She makes a sneeze seem like a splendid event.

Once you let go of your pretensions to adulthood and try to see God's creation through a child's eyes, you may also begin to hear with a child's ears, feel with a child's hands, smell with a child's nose, or taste with a child's tongue. A dog's bark, a piano's chord? Wonderful. How about the feel and smell and taste of bread fresh from the bakery? Incredible. Fantastic. Give me more bread, less angst, about the problems of the world.

I'm not sure why a grandchild moves me to contemplate God's creation more than mothering my four children ever did. Maybe the sleeplessness and hardworking breasts and unending demands of motherhood are too immediate to allow for much contemplative time. Now my daughter meets these urgencies for her daughter, and I sit back and watch the miracle happen. It turns out that my advice is largely useless anyway, as was demonstrated by my recent recommendation of rice cereal for introducing solid foods to a baby. My daughter and my niece, also a new mother, looked at me sadly.

"Not rice," said one.

The other nodded. "Arsenic" was all she said.

They nodded together at this common new-mother knowledge. Wait, what?

Apparently, rice contains traces of arsenic, a fact unknown back in the dark ages of mothering. It's best I stick to reveling in each new discovery my granddaughter makes: sitting up, crawling, pulling herself to standing, ever closer to walking. Her little dynamic body is in constant motion, figuring, assessing, experimenting, growing. She trusts her body's possibilities. She trusts completely in her world's goodness and stability. I know better about the outside world that awaits her; still, I want her trust never to be broken by anyone or anything.

"When I was a child," writes St. Paul in his first letter to the Corinthians, "I used to talk as a child, think as a child, reason as a child; when I became a man, I put aside childish things" (1 Cor 13:11). With apologies to St. Paul, who was never a grandpa, maybe that's our problem. Maybe putting aside childish things boxes us into that jaded, cynical, and unobservant mindset that seems to accompany adulthood. Sometimes I look back and wonder if I was sleepwalking through all those years of parenting my young children. With my eyes only half-open, I worried about illnesses and accidents and every tragedy that could befall my children, but I moved through the everyday unconscious to wonder and awe. I was relieved when they safely outgrew the baby stage, the toddler stage, the elementary school age, and when they'd survived the awkward adolescent stage. They made it through driving, through high school, and through college and safely launched into the world. Then they were adults, battling their own adult challenges—working, marrying, having their own children. They are concerned with big things: with climate change, with democracy, with inequality, with injustice, with making a difference. Having solved little, I have handed over the big worries to them. Now my focus is shrinking.

Where am I going with this? I'm wandering. I'm meandering. I'm feeling my way to the light. I'm going to the place of little relevance known as grandparenting, arriving where the joy of small things with small people is everything. I'm on the road to who-knows-where, and that means everything to me. We like to say that God is in the details, but when I look with the wide-open eyes of a child, I understand the stripped-down theology that God *is* the details, and the details are *amazing*. God's hand winds the lovely cycle of mother-daughter-mother, and we turn with it, full of wonder and awe, full of the grace that greatly resembles paradise.

The parallels between babyhood and old age are striking; at least, they struck me during my recent hip surgery, when my house filled up with the devices necessary for recovery. As I acquired a walker, a cane, a grabber, and other instruments of indignity, I was reminded of the way the furniture for a new baby once accumulated in our house—how the bassinet, the crib, the playpen, and the stroller crowded out the less essential, pre-parenthood gear. As my children grew, the baby necessities were donated.

As I somehow aged from mom to granny, the house was again overtaken: the shower chair replaced the infant tub, the cushion replaced the booster seat. The home rearranging to fit the specialized equipment exists at both ends of life. I worry that soon, younger adults will start to speak to me in that singsong voice and with that stripped-down vocabulary usually reserved for toddlers. I've seen it happen. Hell, I've done it.

When the hospital and rehabilitation center determined that there was nothing more they could do for my dad, he came home for his last weeks of life. By this time his heart was enlarged and pumping at a fraction of its original capability, his kidneys required dialysis (it had been discovered earlier that one of them was shriveled like a raisin left on a vine and had probably never functioned), and his blood was criminally low on platelets. He spent most of the time in the king-size bed in my parents' bedroom, with occasional treks by walker or wheelchair to the bathroom or to thrice-weekly dialysis sessions. My mother had moved to the guest bedroom. Her old bedroom resembled a hospital equipment storage room.

In the midst of the reminders of illness—oxygen tanks and pill bottles and blood pressure machines—my younger sister would do something wonderful every day. Around midmorning, before naptime, she would bring her one-year-old son to visit. While the rest of us often tiptoed around the sickbed, Jonas, in all his blue-eyed, smooth beauty, felt no awkwardness or fear during his time with Grandpa. He would wiggle in my sister's arms until she deposited him at the foot of the bed. He would promptly crawl up to the pillow next to my dad and rest his head next to Grandpa's. Sometimes Jonas reached his little hand out to pet my dad's thin cheek, his way of showing love and compassion. "Gentle," my sister said, but there was no need: Jonas knew instinctively that he was there to give comfort and companionship. He would turn around and change positions and snuggle up anew to Grandpa, like a puppy utterly sure of his adorability and welcome. A few times the caregivers present—the home health aide, the visiting nurse, or the provider of fruitless physical therapy—seemed uneasy with a baby on the patient's bed, but they needn't have worried. Jonas brought only sunshine to a cloudy time.

I have clung for many years to that image of Jonas on Grandpa's bed as a reminder of our earthly span of life. One old man was dying while another young man-child was just beginning to explore the many wonders and riddles his life had yet to offer up to him. Yet the two recognized in each other a kindred spirit. Every day they were so happy to see each other all over again, as though they hadn't seen each other for a long time. Jonas, oblivious to sorrow and pain and worry, gave his grandfather only joy in those wordless moments of communion. I like to think that God finds that kind of joy in us and that whenever we meet God anew in prayer, we have the opportunity for the same experience of welcome and homecoming.

I've also become more mindful of how some folks become more petulant and self-centered as they approach death. As she aged, my mother relieved herself of any responsibility to dispense wisdom; longevity apparently is not synonymous with wisdom. She retreated to the mentality of a toddler being told she couldn't always get what she wanted, actually saying things like "You're not the boss of me!" The wise old crone of lore was nowhere in evidence; instead, she became demanding and manipulative. My father-in-law reacted like a three-year-old to my husband's amateur attempts to care for him physically. Our parents were upset with us for hiring professional caregivers, but they were also irritated by their children's fumbling caregiving. They thrived on being upset. They gave their best energy to being upset. Rather than aging with grace, they regressed with vengeance. They were not the easiest people to love.

Yes, these are lessons I hope to remember for the good of my own children.

I am one of six children, all from the same two parents, but I was officially one of "his" kids, my dad's, according to my mother's estimation. My mom handpicked the three of us she liked best and dubbed them "her" kids, but I was not one of them. My mother was Irish, and I inherited the genetically obvious red hair and freckles, so she said that it took her a while to figure me out. One day she looked at me across the kitchen table. This was after I was already a mother myself. "You're sneaky," she told me, pointing at me thoughtfully with her fork. "You look like one of my kids, and you should be one of mine. But you're one of his through and through."

My mother didn't understand that being one of "his" kids was actually a relief to me. She thought she was taking me down a peg, but it's not like my mother and I ever really had a good appreciation of each other. I was never the daughter she wanted, but fortunately, two of my sisters were (two of "her" kids), so that alleviated some of the disappointment we felt with each other. We loved each other in the way that mothers and daughters are supposed to love each other, but we had no easy camaraderie. Instead, we tiptoed around the land mines we each thought the other had set. I recently came across the breezy message I sent to friends and family after my mother had gotten through her hip replacement:

> Thanks for your prayers—at eighty-three, with Parkinson's and dementia, my mom has come through a broken hip, hip replacement surgery, and a stubborn staph infection. She is no longer a candidate for hospice but is eating pureed food and walking a few steps with her walker, with help. We are looking at hiring a full-time aide, but we should be able to move her

back to her home soon. She is also complaining about every-thing and everyone and is perfectly miserable, bless her heart. I think she'll probably outlive me! Kidding aside, it looks like she'll be able to get back to where she was before the fall. Big relief.

Love to all of you, and thank you again for your prayers and caring hearts

—VALERIE

I remember reading through it before I sent it and feeling like a huge fraud. Reading it years after my mother's death, I still feel like a fraud. When I wrote "kidding aside," I was not kidding. When I wrote "big relief," it was a big lie. I'm now speaking ill of the dead, for which I will surely go to hell, but here I go: my mother was a difficult, uncooperative, and surly patient toward the end of her life. I resented the times I had to leave my family and my work and rush to her latest emergency. All the attention in the world would still not have gratified my mother.

It's not pretty when toddlers are in their eighties.

Lessons, lessons—Lord above, help me take them to heart when it matters.

Perhaps a reminder of my creaking, aging body, a random fainting spell required me to pursue further medical investigation into its cause. I was pretty sure that my collapsing at a university recep-tion, prompted by prolonged standing in a hot room and drink-ing a glass of wine on an empty stomach, had injured my pride more than anything else. But I'd promised the ambulance guys (and how I loathed being the object of such emergency drama) that I'd follow up with my doctor for a checkup and blood work. These exams were followed by an EKG, the setup for which lasted longer than the actual test and which yielded a slip of spidery script indicating a healthy heart. Nevertheless, the doctor wanted more: I was scheduled for an echocardiogram.

A week later, I put on a voluminous cotton gown, soft and faded from a thousand washings, and awaited instructions. The technician, a pale-voiced young woman, explained the process and the instrument that would record my heart's behavior. The gel she applied to facilitate the wand's ultrasound transmission of information suddenly reminded me of previous experiences with this goop: the fetal heartbeat monitor that had detected the early existence of my babies in utero. This time the probe pushed lightly into my chest rather than my belly, seeking not another's heart but my own.

As the whoosh of my heartbeat flooded the darkened room, I, too, was inundated by the memory of those four long-ago heartbeats that were so many times faster than my own. I was transported back to the obstetrician's office and almost palpably back into my younger skin, hearing, for the first time in each pregnancy, the presence of a heartbeat other than mine as it skittered around the room, marveling at the divine cleverness that made possible this miracle of new life, rejoicing and worrying in equal parts for this baby's development into a child to love beyond measure. The technician this day was probably younger than my youngest daughter, and I don't know that she would have understood the lone tear that escaped my left eye as I lay on my left side, breast akimbo, while she charted my heart.

"This must be easier on men," I said in an attempt to bring myself back into the present moment. She looked up with a politely inquiring expression.

"No boob," I said.

"Yes," she said and almost smiled.

My heart appeared as a dark red-black blob on her monitor. The white line clearly visible was my pericardium, which is what she told me when I asked. I'd suspected it was some sort of solidly blocked artery. I'd braced for the evidence of impending death or the need for immediate surgery. That's what I got for watching her work and thinking I knew anything at all about what I could see. I also knew that no matter what she saw on that screen, she'd maintain her practiced and professional poker face.

I left with the echo of past babies on my mind and in my heart.

Two weeks later, I received the emailed verdict from an anonymous cardiologist: "Please inform patient, echocardiogram normal." "Geez, slow down with the technobabble, Doc," I thought. I was glad that I could tell my family that I'd likely be around for a while, that my heart was normal. But I could've sworn I'd felt it break just a little while remembering those four hummingbird heartbeats deep in my womb, safe and sound—the safest I was ever able to keep them.

The Lord will guard your coming and going, both now and forever.

—Ps 121:8

CHAPTER 5

The Politics of Aging

You who are older, it is your right to speak, but temper your
knowledge and do not interrupt the singing. Where there is
entertainment, do not pour out discourse, and do not display
your wisdom at the wrong time.

—Sir 32:3–4

Little can make me feel more ancient than a postcard in the mail,
addressed to me, announcing "Funeral advantage program assists
seniors." The unsolicited offer is made in large, bold print so that
aged eyes can more easily read it. Don't all old folks regularly
check out the large-print murder mysteries from the library? If
the thought of my impending funeral is not attractive enough
to lure me in, the card also offers the valuable booklet called
My Final Wishes. The fine, fine print, which old eyes may not be
intended to read, states that a human representative of a particular insurance company will come to my door with the requested
information.

Oh, kill me now; get it over with already!

The daily contents of my mailbox have become an unpleasant
reminder that I am getting older, that I am on the downslope of

age. AARP, which formerly stood for the American Association of Retired Persons but is now named just plain AARP (sort of like the Artist Formerly Known as Prince), has been sending me fake membership cards—they're only valid if I pay my dues—since before I turned fifty. (I would have loved to retire at fifty, but I was actually starting a new job when I was fifty. I guess I mismanaged my youth, financially speaking.) For $16 a year or, if I'd like to play the odds, $200 for a lifetime membership, AARP will provide me with a magazine subscription, a newsletter, travel discounts, exclusive health offers, and my own lobbyist in Washington (okay, I would actually share the lobbyist with several million other seniors agitating for justice). Each offer of membership—*guaranteed* membership, in case I fear rejection—comes with a free gift, such as a flight bag with a prominent AARP logo or something called a trunk organizer. Old people love the freebies.

I've officially joined an older demographic just by staying alive. Whenever I check the box on a form indicating my age as fifty and older, I suspect that I've become less relevant to marketing research. Or maybe I'm more relevant, but not in the edgy way I was once relevant. I've noticed that my favorite TV show, *Jeopardy!*, is now riddled with commercials for laxatives, unpronounceable prescription medications, and things to try for a leaking bladder. I am nostalgic for pitches for cleaning products and quick meals for large families—things that must no longer concern people my age.

As dismal as it may seem, aging can have its perks. For example, I toured a retirement home, or senior living "village," with my mother. She disliked the idea, but if I were old enough, I'd move there today: for one substantial monthly payment, a resident gets a spacious apartment with a full kitchen, all utilities including cable TV, two meals a day in the classy restaurant, laundry service for bedding and towels, transportation to appointments, guest speakers (a famous character actor was scheduled to drop by and sign his new book), special events (a luau by the pool was next), a variety of classes and daily activities, and field trips. Every employee was solicitous; no concern was too unimportant to address. It seemed like a thoughtful mix of privacy and community. In one day a resident could enjoy a memoir-writing class, a water aerobics session with an instructor, a trip to the nearby mall, a happy hour complete with drinks and appetizers and a live pianist, and a movie in the small theater. Or one could hole up all day with a pint of ice cream and one of those large-print mystery novels from the on-site library. The place made me look forward to getting older.

As I inspected the premises with my mother, I remembered visiting college campuses and dormitories with my daughters. They were oddly similar experiences: the nervousness and excitement at the prospect of a new chapter of life in an unfamiliar setting. My mom was being rushed by a sorority of the elderly that, even at eighty, she was not ready to join. "Everybody here is so old," she stage-whispered at one point. I reminded her it was sort of the deal with moving there.

The tour made me realize that everything is relative, that even if my mail persists in reminding me that I am over the hill, I have some good years left on the outside before the senior living complex will let me move in. The folks there think I am a youngster. Maybe I'm not quite ready for that bonus copy of *My Final Wishes*.

Although, I find large print doesn't seem so unreasonably large these days, especially when regular print has gotten so *small*. And another thing—what is that noise that the kids today call *music*?

Just practicing.

Old folks are a political force when harnessed. We comprise a powerful lobby. The monthly AARP magazine that I now receive with my paid membership has the largest circulation of any magazine in the United States. *Of course* it does, as we retired folks are the ones who still love the luster and feel of an actual magazine. My kids would think I'd lost my mind if I gifted them with a magazine subscription that came in the mail. I, on the other hand, still subscribe to five to six magazines. I read them in bed. I bring them on planes. I donate them to the public library. Sometimes I even write for them.

Not surprisingly, I read (or browse) each new issue of *AARP The Magazine*. A back issue (April/May 2023) offered advice on how to talk to young people—specifically, our adult children. It seems we are to avoid starting any sentence with "When I was your age." We are to bite our tongues and exercise patience, to be constructive in settling arguments, and to remember that it's not about us.

I love that last bit. As I age, I find it easier and easier to let go of the focus. My need to be at the epicenter of every group has lessened, dissipated. I'm happy to sit back and just listen to the conversation billowing around me. I am not up on the latest tweets or dances or songs or TV shows, and I'm okay with that because none of those things really apply to me. I remember feeling frustrated with my parents for not keeping up with the times, with innovations like computers and cell phones, but now I see that the times don't always need us older folks to keep up. We had our times. I do believe it's important to learn new things and try new activities as we get older, but we don't have to be on the cutting edge of every new trend. The cutting edge is not our place anymore, because it's not about us. I need to amend the thing I keep saying about us boomers thinking we're the first to do everything: we have to understand that just as we are not the first, we are also not the last. The unique attribute we boomers can claim is that our childhoods were analog and our adult years are digital. We've seen a lot of wild stuff come into common use. Our life spans straddle two centuries along with two technological realities, which can—and should—give us a useful perspective on aging with grace.

I disagree with the old-person idea that everything was better in the past. It wasn't. I recently heard a talk about how autocratic movements always focus on the past rather than looking forward, so maybe old folks are more susceptible to our ongoing national flirtation with autocracy. If you think you used to have all the power, you want it back.

We elders may thoughtlessly state this trope of everything being better in the past because, as humans, we tend to remember the good times and gloss over the bad. If we didn't, every child would be an only child. Labor is hard. Birth is hard. Parenting is hard. What lunatic would do it all again if the gut-level memories were vivid? I loved being a new mom, but I usually don't remember the days when I felt like I'd scream if I had to read one more picture book to the heavy toddler on my lap. I miss kissing their freshly bathed, warm little cheeks at night, but I don't miss not going to the bathroom without interruption. All this time later, I retain some vestiges of early motherhood: after past years of necessity, I still pee really fast. It's a long-ago survival habit.

Some of us older folks have a lot of power and money and free time, and we don't want to let go of any of it, but it's not about us. We can give our free hours to volunteering for charitable organizations that need our hands and for causes we believe in, but it's not our world anymore. Our time is dwindling. But our vote matters, and we tend to show up to vote. The question is whether we vote selfishly or with an eye to the future we envision for subsequent generations. The things we vote for are the things we bequeath them. The things we don't fix are the problems we leave them. I'm looking at you, climate change. If we don't start voting to protect this fragile blue planet, we will deserve the harsh judgment of posterity.

We have to be wise enough to step aside and let the next generation work the system their way. Down with the gerontocracy!

We have to get private money out of politics, which will make it easier for young people to get elected. We have to make it more feasible for them to stay in public service. We have to return honor to the idea, to the idealism, of serving the common good. We have to cheer young people on, support them, and have their backs, and we have to cede our leadership roles gracefully. We can use our power to educate, our money to donate, and our free time to volunteer, all in service of the causes we support. But we have to let go of the reins.

We boomers grew up with the moon in our eyes. The space race against the Soviets was a formative presence in our lives. My big brother's bedroom was lined with the models he'd built of Mercury, Gemini, and Apollo spacecraft. Nothing in his young life crushed him more than when he learned that his bad eyesight, which we'd all inherited from our dad, would prevent him from becoming an astronaut.

The earliest public event I remember is President Kennedy's assassination. I was a first grader. I will always associate this national trauma with the pre-Thanksgiving ritual of gluing colorful construction-paper finger-feathers onto a traced turkey body/hand. I will never forget the startling tears running down Mrs. Farley's cheeks. After the president's death, the country shared a sacred trust that we would fly Americans to the moon in his honor. Each liftoff, each splashdown, each success, and each failure was a main event in our house, a step to fulfilling that promise.

Apollo 11's touchdown on the moon was a holy moment for us. "The Eagle has landed," came astronaut Neil Armstrong's message from space. It was a normal July night where we lived, but the men in the space suits on our TV were close to heaven. We squinted at the crescent moon in the night sky but could not quite discern those tiny figures or the flag they'd planted. As the summer of 1969 closed out a decade of Vietnam and assassinations and civil unrest and the generation gap, the small step/giant leap onto the moon felt like an affirmation of all that was good about our country.

(I visited the Smithsonian Air and Space Museum in Washington, DC, many years after Apollo 11 and was amazed that the rickety tin can on display had made it to the moon and back. What were those men thinking, trusting their lives to the flimsy technology of that capsule? I guess they believed in space even harder than we did.)

All these decades later, the Apple TV+ show *For All Mankind* has reawakened the child in me. Never mind that the series purposely messes with history and our memories—spoiler alert: in the Apple TV+ version, the Russians beat us to the moon—but the show accurately portrays the baby boomer obsession with the space race. I know: Okay, boomer. We're old. It does surprise me a bit to hear other boomers proclaim *For All Mankind* the best show on television because, in spite of its thrilling start, by subsequent seasons, it's gotten kind of dumb. Note, however, that my boomer husband and I still devour new episodes. Most of the younger people I know are not interested in this show. The young people in my life seem vague and blasé about space stuff. It doesn't speak to them like it does to us.

But we grew up on a steady diet of space exploration. We love everything about space. I am not alone in my disappointment that the United Federation of Planets has not, as was portrayed in our prime-time viewing of *Star Trek*, come to pass in our lifetimes. The United Federation's core creed of interstellar justice and peace and harmony eludes us still. But we boomers remember, even if we do not retain, that lovely sense of idealism that shooting for the moon in real life gave us. I don't know that any of us were ever the same after seeing the photo of ourselves from space: a blue floating marble that was small, fragile, and lonely yet beautiful. We suddenly saw our celestial planet as God sees it—as God sees us.

The space race gave us a jolt of the divine, of something greater than us. Space was the final frontier but also the intimation of a closeness to the eternal, the ineffable. How much more of the unknowable could we know? Or was the appreciation of incredibly wider mystery enough? It may be a stretch to say that space made us believe in God, but the possibilities and potential of space shaped us. We boomers were good at rejecting the religion our parents brought us up in, but we were grounded in the belief in *something*. Some of us as adults have returned to our religious roots. Many of us have not. But the spirituality of space has stayed in our souls. We haven't done a great job of mitigating human-caused harm to our struggling blue marble, but perhaps we can use our later years to lead the movement to heed Pope Francis's call to live "our vocation to be protectors of God's handiwork" (*Laudato Si'*, 217).

The work of NASA has become less magical over the years, but we boomers almost can't help following space developments closely. Skylab, the International Space Station, the shuttle trips and tragedies, the probes, the robotic landings, the photos from faraway telescopes, the dream of making it to Mars—these are the news stories that fascinate us still. How about that report about NASA's Double Asteroid Redirection Test (DART) blowing up an asteroid with a high-speed projectile to knock it off its course? Come on! We remember what happened to the dinosaurs, and we thrill to advances in planetary defense! There's a reason that *Star Trek* spin-offs keep spinning. We are still believers. Our imaginations are lifelong captives of space.

In my early twenties, a man tried to interest me in dating him by promising to get me on the list for the first moon colony. It wasn't a pickup line that worked then, and it definitely wouldn't work now, but it did pique my fancy for a moment. Now I am watching a TV show about fictional women who said yes to that invitation, and I'm wondering what ever happened to that guy. He's probably watching *For All Mankind*. And like all of us boomers, he's remembering a childhood full of giddy promise as we hold on to that fleeting feeling of wonder and awe, that little glimpse of God in all of us.

Old people are known for making a lot of noise in the political arena. If I had to guess, I'd put the average age of the angry-letter writers to my local paper at eighty. I'm only half-kidding. When we had young children, my husband and I moved into a gated community ("Never again!" we've vowed) where the board of directors for the development was mostly composed of retired folks, the ones who have the time to schedule and attend endless meetings about small, inconsequential issues. These elected officials spent a lot of time instigating recall petitions and special elections against each other when they disagreed. Every few months, it seemed, little signs on sticks sprouted on lawns, urging us to reinstate this one or recall that one. We lived there for ten years. The local political climate was tiresome and ridiculous. A younger person would never have run for a position on that cantankerous board. A younger person most likely had a job and kids and a life to live.

We complain more as we get older. We have less patience for the manners and niceties of polite society. We are more self-centered when all we really have to deal with is ourselves. I am not proud of this demographic behavior, and I don't want us to be known for it. But politicians know not to get on the wrong side of the voting power of old people. Look how carefully our federal lawmakers tiptoe around their desired cuts to Social Security or Medicare programs. We have lobbyists who complain for us because we give them money. We even get an extra exemption on our federal taxes just for being over sixty-five. Ageism in society may stand in the way of equal rights for elders, but a movement called ageism, according to the ubiquitous Wikipedia, is an ideology defined as social action leading to "the protection and promotion of the rights of older persons based on the grounds of political, social, and economic principles of identity, dignity, and social justice." We are old folks; hear us roar. Now we need to remember to make some noise for the well-being of our children and grandchildren. May we strive to be as wise as our years would suggest. May we use the blip of time we have left for more constructive endeavors.

In addition to the free hours we can devote to volunteering for the causes we feel called to support, the pandemic has pointed out and solidified another essential job for older folks: we are the critical sustainers of artistic culture. We may not be the creators of art anymore, but we are the patrons. I realized this recently from my personal experience as a theatergoer. My husband and I are devotees and supporters of the Oregon Shakespeare Festival, a venerated institution of traditional and innovative annual theatrical productions in Ashland, OR. We see as many plays as possible there every year. Wherever we live, we try to attend local community theater productions, although our combined theater degrees can make us (read: me) snobbish in our critiques.

We haven't always been such benevolent benefactors of the arts. In the years when we were raising four kids, we rarely managed to get out to see a play or a movie or a concert. If we did, we brought the kids with us to give them an appreciation for culture. Sometimes it was popular culture; we saw many of the Disney animated movies on their first run. But we also took the kids to matinee or preview performances of live theater when the tickets were cheaper. We visited museums wherever we went, usually when we were visiting family and, most fortuitously, on the random days when entry was free to the public. My husband gamely took teenagers to concerts by bands they adored. (A memorable example of this is when, once upon a time, he was the only dad standing at the back of a Blur concert in Hollywood, trying not to look out of place.) As time went on, a lot of the plays and dance concerts and music recitals we attended were because our kids were performing in them.

Once our baby birds fledged from the nest, we had more leisure time and available income to be audience members. Then the pandemic shut down live performances of all kinds: theater, opera, dance, readings, concerts, exhibits, sports—every event that required a gathering of humans to be viable. The show did not go on. Three years later, the show is having a hard time going on, as most institutions have hemorrhaged their meager rainy-day funds and are in limited operation, having lost the revenue of paying audiences for three seasons.

Now the organizations and companies of artists who bring us joy, challenge our preconceptions, and feed our souls need our help.

My husband and I have noticed over the past decade or so— not coincidentally, the time of our lives when we've been able to afford tickets to plays—that the audiences that include us tend to look like us: lots of older white people. We are the patrons because we have some disposable income. It pains me that the institutions of performing and visual arts, essential to civilization and expression, are often reduced to relying on the contributions they must beg from people like us. But until charitable foundations and/or government programs step up to fund artists and artistic endeavors, we are it. If we are lovers of theater, not only must we attend and support productions wherever and whenever we can, we must find innovative ways to make it possible for people, especially young people and young families and students of all ages, to indulge in live performances at affordable prices or even for free. A person's first unfolding of Shakespeare is a wondrous thing. Never underestimate the magic of live theater—of the power of words and music, of costumes and sets, of actors and their passion—to touch us deeply and viscerally, to challenge and change us.

The pandemic sent us all scrambling for the comforts of home, by which I mean a well-equipped and insulated home that we need never leave, especially for entertainment purposes. We cocooned ourselves. We wanted to live "in security, everyone under their own vine and fig tree," as the Bible says (1 Kgs 5:5), but that is not a healthy overall trend for society. We watched movies at home on the widest TV screen that would fit in the family room, but we are not returning to the movie theaters in a hurry, much like we are not going back in adequate numbers to live performances.

I would be so sad if going to the movies were to become a relic of the past, like the loss of the drive-in movies of my childhood. I have always loved going to the movies. I love the anticipation before the lights go down. I love picking seats. I love the previews. I love the snacks. I love the hush falling over the crowd when the movie starts. I love the sense of community with the other audience members in the dark, the laughing and gasping of strangers all reacting to the action on the screen at the same time. My cousin, an avid moviegoer, once likened his time in a movie theater to a reverent visit to a cathedral. Movies are his religion. I wouldn't go quite that far. But I missed the movies terribly during the COVID-19 years. I've only gone back recently and am still mindful of infection, still wary of people coughing in a closed space.

The pandemic has shown us that normal life can disappear in a heartbeat, and a grim new normal can deprive us of all we have taken for granted, all we cherish—even our livelihoods and our loved ones. A cautious return to anything that was once familiar, even something as inconsequential as a movie, is cause for joy.

Even if we are not patrons of the arts, season ticket holders to sports teams, or annual pass subscribers to the zoo, our money can support the businesses we care about in small ways. I've always wanted to write a short story about a customer who is known to all the baristas at an independent coffee shop as Old Man Mocha, so named because he orders the same drink every morning. Like much fiction, this is based on a true story, as was told to me by one of my barista kids. Whoever worked the opening shift looked forward to seeing Old Man Mocha every morning, as though his presence meant that the world was still turning and everything was all right, at least for that day. Old Man Mocha was a kind person and a consistent tipper. He made a difference he will never know.

⚜

"You're having a sandwich at 12:15?"

I am incredulous. My husband has rocked my world. He's eating lunch early.

How fast it has happened: we've retired, and now lunch is at one o'clock, no exceptions, now and forever, amen.

I guess we thought that when we left jobs that dictated our lunch hour and, by extension, our breakfast and dinner times, the jobs would leave us. It turns out that the lack of structure inherent in retirement begs for a schedule. We eat lunch at one. We shop for groceries in the morning. We plan our dinners for the week. We say it is because we are attempting not to waste precious food, that we want to finish the fresh ingredients in creative ways, but is it perhaps that we secretly like the comfort and security of knowing what's for dinner?

I can blame our mealtime rigidity on job history, or I can face the fact that as we get older, we harden. Our arteries harden, our brain synapses harden, our beliefs harden, and our hearts harden. New inventions, which used to delight us, now intimidate us—not all of us, as I imagine some inventors do good work in their later decades. My husband is still enthralled by innovations in technology, like the latest smartphone connected to the latest smartwatch. I, on the other hand, am paralyzed when I am forced to update my phone or my laptop. If I were single, I might still be using a typewriter.

Age and habit can harden our hearts into stone. Anatomically, a hardened heart is not a healthy heart. When the arteries harden due to blockage, the function of communication among the various parts of the heart is impaired or lost. Metaphorically, a hardened heart does not work as intended. It has rather put up barriers and erected defensive lines around itself. If we've hardened our hearts, we aren't receptive to new insights or ideas or feelings.

"I will remove the heart of stone from your flesh and give you a heart of flesh," the Lord tells his people via the prophet Ezekiel (Ez 36:26). We older folks, who are set in our ways, need to remember what it feels like to have a heart of flesh and blood, to live each day with a heart that feels deeply, a heart that bleeds for the pain of others. We have to get it out of our heads that all is well as long as we wake up without a backache and lunch is at one.

We need to imagine how our hearts might feel if we weren't sure whether our young children would survive or die trying to live on an uninhabitable planet because our elders had ignored the warning signs and failed to act. Imagine if our grandparents in the last century had closed their eyes and hardened their hearts and allowed fascism to take over our country: we would blame them for not keeping us safe and free. We would deplore their lack of foresight in losing this once-great democracy. We would doubt they ever cared about us or about anything beyond themselves.

We're the grandparents now.

We need to stop wringing our hands about the unrecognizable mess the world has become and act on behalf of our grandchildren and their grandchildren. We may not be able to join the military or run for office or even march very far with a protest sign, but we can make the signs. We can write and debate. We can talk and text. We can educate and persuade. We can be *age appropriate*. We can massage our hardened hearts back into pliant flesh.

Similarly, if we have occupied elected office for many years, we have to check on the health of our minds and hearts. A job we once did with ease may be too much to ask of us now. A judge or a senator in their nineties may command respect for the work they have done, but the realities and ravages of aging may indicate that it's time to step down. A graceful exit is better than a confused and overdue departure. It is a difficult topic to broach with an elder statesperson, but it is often a necessary one.

Our hardened hearts can sometimes tell us that no one will ever be able to do our job adequately, to fill our shoes. History shows this to be untrue, as does this personal history: I once imagined I was irreplaceable. My solution was to find the perfect replacement so that I could I go elsewhere with peace of mind. I left that job in what I thought were good hands. My replacement had worked alongside me and knew how everything should run. I was confident that every program I had started would continue without a hitch. "I hope I don't mess up," my replacement wrote in a farewell card from the whole staff, which should have given me pause. Within a short time, I heard that my handpicked replacement had been let go for having broken a bunch of workplace rules and perhaps a law. All of my precious programs were out of commission. But the lesson for me was not that I was irreplaceable, it was that I had failed in my choice of replacement. I could only hope that the departure of my replacement led to an opening for an unknown person with young blood and fantastic ideas to take over and *rule* that job.

Our goals and values change along with our politics as we age, but among my friends and family who are my age and older, I see that the folks who are comfortable in their own skin have hearts that have become fleshier instead of more hardened. They see the nuance of gray area where they once saw only black and white. They embrace the new while not holding too tightly to the old. They speak and act with a hard-won sense of perspective. It's a delicate balancing act, this getting older.

It is our job as the wise old people to care about the safety and well-being of the young, even if we don't quite understand them. It is our job to look to and protect a future that we will not share in, and to vote accordingly. The political matters that no longer seem to affect us—just wages, environmental regulations, reproductive health rights, fair government representation, marriage equality laws, criminal justice reform—are even more important for us to continue to espouse and support, because this old world will not end when we do.

They shall bear fruit even in old age.

—Ps 32:15

Some Physical and Mental Realities of Aging

Moses was one hundred and twenty years old when he died, yet
his eyes were undimmed and his vigor unabated.

—Dt 34:7

My husband and I spend a fair amount of time trying to diagnose our ailments by using reasoning and deduction rather than
by running to the doctor. On a recent Thursday, my husband is
convinced that eating an orange has made his gums sore. "Am I
going to have to give up oranges?" he asks, his regret evident. It
is the height of orange season, and the produce section is bright
with navels, cara caras, blood oranges, satsumas, mandarins, tan-
gelos, Minneolas, tangerines; pyramids of citrus are beckoning,
threatening to tumble. We shared a sweet, juicy orange the night
before. Now his gums are tender.

I tell him not to rush to judgment. I tell him maybe to let his
gums heal and then to try another bite of orange. I say that if my
back hurts the day after we have sex, even if I suspect the cause
might be the sex, I'm not going to stop having it. I'm just going

to be more careful. I'm going to give myself a few days to shake it off. The comparison may or may not be apt.

But we are in our midsixties. Our bodies have been with us for the long haul, and we have not always treated them kindly. When I was young, I didn't know I'd have to take such thoughtful care of my body. I never imagined that there would come a day when a series of jumping jacks would tear the meniscus in my knee. I didn't even know my knee contained something called a meniscus. I must have noticed that my grandparents moved slowly and groaned when they got up from the couch, but I never imagined being a grandparent. I thought running and lunging and twisting and squatting would always be as effortless as they were at the time. Now that I have to monitor myself, I miss that thoughtlessness of movement. I had a vague idea of aging, but the numbers were nonsensical. I remember doing the math, perhaps in 1967, that when the turn of the century came, I would turn forty-three that year, which sounded so old that I figured I might as well be dead as still alive in the year 2000. Surely, life would no longer be enjoyable at that advanced age. There was no point in even entertaining the prospect of reaching such an age. Now forty-three seems positively springlike.

Conversely, I also remember marveling at the resilience of the human body when each of my parents was dying slowly. My dad's internal organs were valiant as they kept up a feeble appearance of functioning. My mom's brain kept up her shallow breathing long after her consciousness fled. I remember looking at those ravaged bodies in the weeks before they died and thinking, How? How is this poor body still alive? As much as I didn't want my parents to die, I was devastated by their visible diminishment. The human body is stubborn, but the will to keep it alive is the fiercest force of nature. It awes me still.

My husband and I try to outgame the aging system with many tricks. We think we are owed some time because we quit smoking all those years ago. We give up meat. We buy whole wheat bread and pasta. We take the stairs. We drink less alcohol. We give up drinking. We drink more water. We drink only water. We face the ticking clock of our life span as though logic applies, as though we don't know the conflicting stories of very fit runners who drop dead at forty and centenarian two-pack-a-day smokers, as though we can bend the randomness of life into a rational shape. We should know better.

It hardly matters that eating an orange may not have made my husband's gums sore or that the way we had sex may not have tweaked my back, because we perceive these to be reasonable conclusions of cause and effect. Now we can enjoy the comfort and triumph of having *figured it out*. It must be the orange. It makes sense. It must be the sex position. What else could it be? Never mind that every pang and pain could be a lot of things. We congratulate ourselves. It feels good to have solved the mysteries of sex and oranges.

As a public service, I'm always happy to use my life experience— my *many years* of life experience—to help others. Today's lesson is "How not to live a life in the sun, especially if your melanin is minimal."

Melanin is a natural pigment in the top layer of skin that determines skin and hair color. It is light absorbent and helps protect our skin from sun damage. But melanin can't do it alone. Dermatologists recommend commonsense precautions to safeguard one's skin against the harm of ultraviolet (UV) radiation: Avoid outdoor activities during the middle of the day, even if the sky is cloudy. Choose a broad-brimmed hat and protective clothing when you go outdoors. Use sunscreen year-round whenever you are outside, and reapply it every two hours. Wear sunglasses. Avoid tanning beds, which use artificial UV rays. Inspect your skin (all your skin, even the unmentionable parts) for any growths or changes to moles or freckles.

I admit I have not done a lot of these things, but a persistent sore on my thigh that just wouldn't heal led to a referral to a dermatologist.

"Tell me about your history in the sun," the dermatologist suggested.

I figured I'd start with the sunburns. I told him how, when I was a freckle-faced kid spending summer weeks with my grandparents at the Jersey shore, my siblings and I got our first good sunburn of the season on purpose. We returned from our first day at the beach looking like boiled crabs. Once we'd suffered through the night of pain and chills and been coated with the paste of Noxzema, and once our angry skin had peeled, we were good to go, pronounced immune from sunburn for the rest of the summer. Our hair lightened, our freckles darkened, and our fair skin sort of tanned.

Back home at the public pool, we were similarly unprotected. My mother slathered baby oil onto her exposed skin and put little plastic spoons over her eyes while she sunbathed; I remember the oil floating on the water when she dipped into the shallow end to cool off. We fried ourselves, oblivious of anything called sunscreen. Sometimes my mother dabbed us with suntan lotion, like the little girl on the Coppertone billboards, but it was almost an afterthought. Summer and sunburn went together.

That was my childhood.

The dermatologist listened to me with a bit of horror but also with a look that said he'd heard this story before from people my age. Then he proceeded to investigate every inch of my skin. A nurse with an iPad took photos on his cue. This felt like some kind of special humiliation for the elderly, but it was done swiftly and professionally. The doctor used what looked like a fancy can of whipped cream (actually liquid nitrogen) to freeze off some of the little barnacles he found growing on my epidermis.

A biopsy officially confirmed that I had skin cancer, or basal cell carcinoma. Basal cell and squamous cell are the two most common forms of skin cancer. They are also called nonmelanoma skin cancers, with melanoma being a far deadlier diagnosis. The treatment was that the weird spot, actually a cluster of cancerous cells, had to be removed.

"So we'll take care of your first skin cancer today," the dermatologist said at my next visit. The way he'd said "first" made me realize that the repercussions of my boiled-crab childhood were unlikely to end with this appointment, because basal cell carcinoma usually recurs. The doctor pricked around the problem area with lidocaine and then explained that he was scraping away the cancer like you'd scrape out the rotten spot on a raw potato before cooking the remaining firm part of it—a rather nauseating image of decay to associate with one's limb. I went home with a perfect circle resembling a bullet hole on my leg. Now it is healing, although the darkened mess left behind will most likely take its time fading. My dermatologist plans to check my whole body every year for further eruptions. I can hardly wait.

So, friends, listen to your dermatologist.

I like to think that, as a mother, I was better at covering my own children with sunscreen when we went swimming, as they freckle like I do. But I could have been more committed to their safety. I only hope skin cancer is not in their future. I conclude this small life lesson with the observation that, as much as we swear that we are not going to be like our parents, we are sometimes a lot like our parents—right down to our skin.

My husband and I are less than two years apart (he is the youngster), so we are fortunate to be aging together. Still, I wonder sometimes if this is the best arrangement because we are starting to be suspicious of one another. Take, for example, the cheese grater. It's a normal four-sided tin grater with a handle, and we've had it for years. But it's missing. The last time I wanted to grate some cheese, I couldn't find it. It was gone. I searched every kitchen cabinet. I asked my husband if he'd seen it, and it turned out that he'd wanted to use it several days before and had been unable to find it. He'd searched every cabinet. Together, we searched again. We searched through other cabinets in other rooms in the house. The grater has yet to turn up. I'm going to buy another one, which will surely make it appear.

We joke about its whereabouts, but I think each of us is secretly worried that we will find it somewhere crazy, like in the car or behind the couch, and we'll realize with a sinking heart that our spouse is losing it, that we'd always remember this day as the beginning of the end of our spouse's mental faculties, when one of us would officially become a caregiver.

We ease the tension with a running joke we crack when one of us does something clueless or absentminded: "Don't tell the kids," the errant one of us says to the other. It's a play on what you say to your siblings when you're a kid and you've done something wrong: "Don't tell Mom." I said it recently when I realized I'd worn my leggings inside out all day. We joke that we have to keep each other's secrets because if the kids find out we're senile, they'll have us committed to the old folks' home. For now the kids are in on the gag. We can only trust that when the time comes, they will give us the grace advised by the sage author of Sirach regarding one's father: "Even if his mind fails, be considerate of him" (Sir 3:13). I'm hoping that goes for the mother too.

One day we are driving through a city to go somewhere new, but as I'm looking out the car window, I have a sudden feeling and think, "We've been here before." It's not déjà vu but a vague and buried memory. I say this to my husband, but he is unconvinced.

He doesn't find it familiar. Slowly, painstakingly, I snatch each detail as it floats up into my conscious brain: "We were picking something up. You parked and I stayed in the car. It was raining." I say each sentence carefully, like I am a medium at a séance receiving messages from the beyond. Suddenly, the light dawns in his eyes. My husband remembers the day I'm talking about as well. We have been here before! It just took a while to retrieve the buried data.

I feel like I've been panning for gold, sifting through the water and rocks and silt and junk in the stream of my memory until I find the little nuggets of past experience. Remembering that street is about as profitable as panning for gold, but I am satisfied, if worn out, with this day's work. I guess this is how it's going to be.

I'm finding that my age is becoming the most medically pertinent thing about me. It recently came up during an appointment to schedule a hip replacement.

"Hip replacements last twenty to twenty-five years," my doctor said. "So—"

He broke off suddenly, a stricken look on his unlined face.

"So that should do it?" I said, finishing his thought.

He looked at me helplessly.

"I get it," I said. "I'm sixty-five. You're saying I won't have any need to replace the replacement?"

When I smiled, he smiled: situation defused.

My doctor is a young man, so I harbor no hard feelings toward him. I appreciate the clear and unhurried way he explains my medical choices to me. His discomfort was not mine, because I am realizing, in my first year of Medicare eligibility, that the endgame is going to require a good and sturdy sense of humor.

Medicare, having coincided with my move to a new state and the gradual easing of COVID-19 fears, has enabled me to catch up on all the routine health measures I had let slide. For example, I made an appointment for a Pap smear with a new gynecologist.

"Right," she said. "So we no longer require screening for cervical cancer for women over sixty-five." She had the same habit of speech my daughters employ, which is their beginning tricky sentences with "So."

"I had no idea," I said.

"So it's just that the incidence of cervical cancer is so low that the screening doesn't make sense. So this will be your last Pap smear!" She said this like it was a great joy—as it should be.

"Yay," I said. But I didn't feel especially festive, which was weird. I would have thought that my last date with the speculum would be cause for elation. But again, here it was: the endgame. My age seemed to have a life of its own—a finite life.

I think I am at peace with being a senior citizen. A boomer. A retiree. I love my flexible schedule and my 10 percent discounts and my calm perspective. But the person I see in the mirror is suddenly not the elder person others see. Sure, I see the signs of the years I've lived. But I have yet to see a little old lady. I don't see my grandmother. I don't see *a* grandmother. I see a fighter. I see an age warrior.

Still, I have developed a morbid interest in the causes of death listed in the obituaries of famous people if they are in their sixties. An actor dies at eighty-five? Sure. An author dies at ninety-three? Reasonable. A musician dies at sixty? Hold on . . . why? What disease or what cancer happened? What part gave out? I will scroll through an entire obituary to get to the cause of death of this person who seemed too young to die. I need to know all the tragic things that can happen to kill a sixty-year-old. I feel cheated when a cause of death is not given. My tracking of obituaries reminds me of a cartoon I once saw of a man reading the paper and the headlines above the individual obituaries are things like "Ten

Years Older" or "Five Years Younger" or—the one I dread—"Exactly Your Age." Apparently, I am not alone in perusing this section of the paper with personally applicable interest.

I remember back when I was fifty-one, I overheard a coworker groan, "My dad is turning *fifty* this weekend. He's getting so old." It was perhaps the first time I faced the fact that while I think of age as just a number, those same numbers as seen through the eyes of a younger person are just old.

I confess to personal vindication when some medical professional, filling out my chart on their handy floating computer, asks me, "What medications are you on?" Note that they no longer ask me if I am on any medications but, rather, are poised to type in which medications I am on, as I am surely on several at my age. "None," I say, and the look of astonishment, quickly masked, makes me happy. There's life in the old girl yet.

On a good day, I can decide to embrace my age, my worn-out hip, my unchecked cervix, my birth year that is found miles down the online drop-down menu. On a bad day, I feel sorry for my old self. But I could have said similar things when I was a teenager: On a good day, I can embrace my acne, my fickle period, my lack of long legs or cool clothes. On a bad day, I feel sorry for my unfinished self.

In the months before I turned sixty, I had to stop doing what I thought of as morbid math: I'd think, "When I am sixty, if I live to be eighty, I will have already lived three-quarters of my life. When I am sixty, if I live to be ninety, I will have already lived two-thirds of my life." I figured eighty is a ripe old age and ninety is a long shot, so the odds are that I had already lived most of my life. "That went awfully fast," I'd think. But, as Shakespeare's poor Lear says, "O, that way madness lies" (*King Lear*, III, iv, 24).

As it turned out, the buildup to turning sixty was worse than the actual event. Getting to sixty was a thrilling ride. I've lived in fascinating times, having been born in the same year as Sputnik. I spent my childhood in a nation reaching for the moon. In my lifetime I have been a witness to the most amazing discoveries and technologies and developments. The world has changed drastically and dizzyingly in the past six decades. Dear world, we've had some wild times, you and me.

The road may go on and on, but with apologies to the hobbits, the individual journey does not. Sixty is a slowing in the rate of travel, but sixty has also invited me to look around a little more instead of focusing on the route ahead. There is beauty everywhere if we ease up and notice. There is much to ponder, much to wonder about, and much to love.

And there are benefits. Menopause, when you are finally through the messy transitional part, actually rocks. What could be better than never having to worry about an unplanned pregnancy or passing by the array of feminine products at the grocery store and not needing any? I'd hate to count up the fortune I'd spent during my fertile years on tampons and the like. I spend my savings now on anti-wrinkle creams and vitamins.

I, at sixty-something, am much more likely to speak my mind. I now have no problem looking someone straight in the eye and saying, "Of course you know I completely disagree with you." At fifty, I would have sugarcoated that statement, and at forty or in any earlier decade, I would have kept my opinion to myself. After sixty, I don't have to impress anyone, retreat from anyone, or act like I agree with anyone when I don't. I'm in my sixties; I don't have a lot of time left!

Actually, my sixties feel pretty much like my late fifties. I'm at peace with the creaking bones in the morning and the getting up to pee at night, with the crow's-feet framing my eyes and the descent of the valiant breasts. I have earned these features, after all. I can't expect to look younger than my children. I'd just rather look a little less like my own grandma.

Aging may be the great equalizer of society's strata. I thought about this when I worked in the library of a state prison. The yard where I worked was medium security, and a large number of the inmates who frequented the library were lifers, meaning that they'd been in prison for a long time. Most of them were serving a term of some years to life rather than life without parole, so they had the prospect of being released, albeit as old men. Most of them had outgrown their inclination to break the law. They were just trying to get along and maybe go home.

Before I worked in a prison, I expected the cells to be full of scary, dangerous tough guys. Imagine my surprise when a lot of the book requests I got from these older prisoners concerned health issues. They wanted up-to-date information on prostate health and heart disease and arthritis. They were more interested in lowering their cholesterol than in bomb making. I realized that they were dealing with the same challenges of aging that all seniors deal with, whether we are billionaires or poor, free or incarcerated, educated or illiterate, male or female, black or white or brown. They might have done some terrible things and spent their most productive years in prison, but they were subject to the same physical wear and tear, the same breakdown of the body, that we all face in our golden years.

Some of the men tried to be as healthy as possible under the circumstances. The younger men worked out or played basketball or other sports; the older ones walked the track, sometimes slowly, often for hours. Some of them had spent a lifetime damaging their bodies with drugs and/or alcohol. Some prisoners combated their addictions by attending twelve-step programs, although some continued their substance abuse on the sly. The food in state prison is configured to provide large groups of people with the minimum nutritional requirements at a minimal cost, so many men supplemented their diets with items they could buy at the commissary or supplies they could order—or their families could send them—in quarterly packages from approved vendors. Very little of the food in prison was fresh or flavorful. One of the library clerks gave me some solid health advice he'd gleaned over his years of incarceration: when you prepare a packet of ramen or a cup of noodles, only use half of the high-sodium seasoning packet. What that nugget of information told me was that grown men were subsisting indefinitely on an impoverished-college-student diet.

The medical care the prisoners received from the state was perfunctory at best, even though it consumed a large slice of the prison budget. Behind bars it was hardly the gold-plated health care that one reads about in sensationalized and/or fact-free op-eds. Whether a prisoner had high blood pressure or a possible separated shoulder, Tylenol was the miracle drug with which he usually left the clinic. No one was getting free knee replacements without a ton of demonstrable damage and pain.

Many of the men with whom I worked did go home eventually. They usually went first to transitional homes, which were places where they could catch their breath and learn how to ease back into society. They had to figure out cell phones and ATM cards and online job applications. They were often starting entry-level work that was physically hard on the body. Many of them became long-distance truck drivers. They took their old-man health problems with them out into the free world. Nature does not discriminate.

A friend posted a Tibetan proverb on Facebook: "The secret to living well and longer is: Eat half, walk double, laugh triple, and love without measure." As social media has taught us, it is possible the quote may be neither Tibetan nor a proverb, but it stabs my heart a little—at least, the part about walking double does. Due to osteoarthritis in my right hip, my walking has been curtailed recently.

This makes me sad. I love to walk. As my decades have progressed, I've gone from being a committed dancer to an indifferent runner to a stationary cyclist, but I've always been a walker. I love a good hike either alone or with company. The miles feel good. The world is beautiful. I've always thought of walking the dog as daily therapy to clear out my brain. I've taken my ability to walk—my feet, legs, knees, and hips in smooth cooperation, oiled cogs in my biological machine—for granted.

I could blame my mother's brittle Irish bones for my condition, but let's face it, my age has more to do with the breakdown of my hip. Over the years we wear away the cartilage that cushions the moving parts of our joints. No one tells us that this precious cartilage does not replenish itself. It cannot be restored or fabricated or grown in a lab—at least, not yet. Once we lose it, we experience pain in the joint. Eventually, we arrive at the need for surgical replacement.

That's where I'm at. I tried a steroid injection, which seemed miraculous for a time—look at me, I can bend and walk and dance and kneel again! But those effects gradually wore off. Subsequent injections will likely be less effective with each dose. Surgery is in my future if I want to keep walking.

For now I try to ignore the pain. I try to carry on with life within my limits. I go about my daily activities with a thought to which ones are going to hurt and how to ration my energy to get the most done before my hip can no longer be ignored. I creak like an old house in the morning, and I need a few minutes to relearn how to walk after a long car ride. As I navigate the mazes of health insurance costs and surgical options, I set my course for a hip replacement.

And all shall be well. My doctor says I am a good candidate, and my surgeon cites a 96 percent success rate. ("What's the deal with that 4 percent?" I wonder silently. I don't want that statistic to include me.) I will have to get a cane and a walker for my weeks of recovery time, which will include physical therapy and good pain meds. My husband will have to cater to my needs (the "for worse" part of our vows, my poor darling). I will heal. I will hike again—I hope.

I've long dreamt of walking the width of Spain on the popular pilgrimage known as the Camino de Santiago, or the Way of St. James. I consider this eight-hundred-kilometer trek to be the ultimate experience of walking as spiritual journey. The walk is physical; the progress of faith, symbolic. You take five weeks to walk west through Spain to the Atlantic Ocean, traveling through bad weather and blisters, relying on the kindness of strangers and the camaraderie of fellow hikers—fellow searchers—on the trail. It's my kind of walk. It was one of my retirement goals. Then COVID-19 and then the hip delayed all travel plans.

My doctor told me to keep walking in moderation but to avoid hills. If only he could see the giant hill that is my driveway that I'd been power walking up and down every day, thinking it was good for me. He told me to limit high-impact exercise, probably like the series of jumping jacks in my workout routine. The activities I thought were good for me have turned out to be bad for my impoverished cartilage. My doctor told me to swim. I am so *not* a swimmer. I hardly recognize this less-active person I'm supposed to become, and that's before I glimpse the crone in the mirror.

I'm too hard on myself, I know. But also, perhaps I'm too grandiose: a boomer who is somehow the first human ever to age and must document the details, right? My hip is hardly unique in the annals of aging. We grow old, and we deal with it. I worry that the left hip will go next and then each knee, followed by every joint that is put in and shaken all about for the hokey pokey, all eventually needing surgery. I worry I will spend much of my remaining life waiting to walk again.

Walking the walk has always been my metaphor of choice for growing closer to God, for following the path to a sturdier faith, for keeping my feet on holy ground. Who am I if I am unable to walk? Maturity has become a lesson I don't particularly want to learn. The breakdown of physical and mental ability is surely leading me somewhere, but do I want to follow that map? I think of Jesus's words toward the end of the Gospel of John: "Amen, amen, I say to you, when you were younger you used to dress yourself and go where you wanted; but when you grow old, you will stretch out your hands, and someone else will dress you and lead you where you do not want to go" (Jn 21:18). This is traditionally thought to be a reference to the way St. Peter would be martyred. I used to think of my parents when I heard this Gospel read at Mass and how, at the end of their lives, they needed intimate assistance from their children but complained about it mightily. Now the verse seems more personally pertinent. "Yikes," I think. Age is definitely leading me to where I do not want to go.

But whether I want to go there or not is beside the point, isn't it? And I'm not there yet. I can still dress myself and go where I want to go. Giving in to moaning about my bad hip may be premature surrender. I can still walk. I just have, as the cowboys say, a hitch in my giddyup. I still have blessings that will take me forever to count. I have health insurance that will provide a new hip, even as this old one has given me a fresh appreciation for the miracle of each blooming day.

Maybe the secret to aging gracefully is understanding that we've already made a lifetime of progress on our spiritual walk. We can't stop time, but we can befriend it and be kind to it rather than race against it. We can just keep putting one old, trudging foot in front of the other. We may have to slow our pace on our walk to God's finish line. We're going to get there all the same.

Finally, after several postponements and a cancellation, when my husband is available to care for me (after caring for his dying father to the end) and when the stars have aligned, my hip replacement surgery gets scheduled. It is preceded by presurgery appointments and evaluations and X-rays, checks on my vital signs, and a class. It's an actual lecture in a classroom, although my fellow attendees are not all there for hips. Some are knees, some are shoulders, but we are none of us what you would call able-bodied. Most of us are older, but a few are surprisingly young. They've had work-related or sports-incurred injuries rather than the garden-variety ravages of time. We each bring home a spiral-bound binder full of information that is fifty-five pages long, with sections like "Common Causes of Hip and Knee Problems," "Hip Joint and Knee Joint Replacement Surgery," "Before Surgery," "Home Safety Checklist," "Day of Surgery," "During Surgery," "Recovery," "Returning Home," "Exercise and Mobility," and "Life after a Joint Replacement." We're told that we'll be consulting this book often once we leave the class and once we are home and healing. The hospital staff has obviously done this prep many times before.

Heather, our teacher, is a nurse who makes herself available day and night to her surgery patients. She is the one I will call with every question in the days following my surgery, and she will always get back to me. Nurse Heather is the talkative member of the team, as my surgeon is the quiet one. Everyone else speaks of him glowingly, but he only speaks on a need-to-know basis. His right-hand man, the physician's assistant, takes the time to explain to me, using props, the long titanium bar that will be inserted into my femur and the synthetic ball atop it that will fit into the synthetic cup that will replace my worn-out hip joint once they've removed the old arthritic ball. It sounds preposterous, and there are risks, as with any surgery, but it mostly works.

For the week before my surgery date, I have to stop taking the naproxen that has been getting me through each day. The rationing of my daily activities becomes even more stringent. I know it's going to get worse before it gets better, but I am hopeful that the pain that's accompanied me all day for a while—from my rising in the morning to sleeping at night—will be ending.

On the morning of my surgery, I don't eat or drink. I shower from the chin down with antibacterial soap, paying special attention to my hip. I pack stretchy clothes to accommodate any post-surgical swelling ("No skinny jeans," says Nurse Heather). I pack toiletries I won't use. I pack books I won't read. We have to get to the hospital so early that when we arrive, the main entrance is still locked and we have to enter through the emergency room, a walk that looms like a long one for me (it isn't, really) around the building. My husband stays with me through the preliminary paperwork and physical prep (the vitals, the IV, the unflattering hospital gown), but then he must leave. He takes my wedding ring with him. I know he is a worrier, and I know he is off to worry in a waiting room for a few hours. They tell him he can go else-where, but I'm pretty sure he won't. I wish I could set his mind at ease—I'm not worried—but I know I can't.

I explain to the anesthesiologist that I have a history of being very hard to knock out, and I don't want to remember any of this time under the knife, and he reassures me. "My wife is a redhead," he says, which puts me at peace: he is fully aware that many red-heads (like me) are weirdly resistant to anesthesia. My last memory before losing all memory of these hours is of being rolled onto my side to expose and stabilize the right hip that will be replaced, as well as my thinking, "I am a ham"—an actual ham, a big ham to be expertly carved. This mental image is indelible. Then I am out.

I wake in the recovery area to those loud nurses who insist on waking you after surgery and whom you wish would just go away and let you sleep. Another X-ray is taken, and I pray everything took. After I emerge from the fog of unknowing, they wheel me to my room. I see my husband in the hallway, smiling at me with so much love, and I burst into tears. I don't know why. The nurse kindly blames the effects of anesthesia. "I'm not sad," I say as I cry extravagantly. "I'm not sad"—just emotional, apparently.

I've planned to stay only one night, but I take them up on the option to stay for two. The staff get me up and walking (or halting) pretty soon after surgery, but my problem, more than the pain, is the pain medication. It makes me not only nauseous but also unable to keep anything down. They give me antinausea medication. They also give me meds to take home to counteract the constipation caused by the pain meds. I remember watching the series *Dopesick* about the despicable Sackler family's scourge of Oxycontin, and I wonder where the fun part of taking opioids is. Where is the initial fun that leads to addiction? Because I'm not having fun. I have to throw up in the wastebasket during my first physical therapy session, which is hardly pleasant for my poor therapist. My first call to Nurse Heather after I'm home is to ask if I can stop taking the pain medication, which requires using the other medications, none of which are working. I'm hungry, but I can't eat. I'm tired of vomiting nothing. "Sure, if you can handle the pain with just aspirin and Tylenol," she says. I find that I can. I can also eat and poop like a normal person. I ask Nurse Heather how I will know if I've dislocated my new hip—the one thing you never, ever want to happen. "You'll know because you'll be here in the emergency room," she says. It would be that painful. I am so careful not to fall; I use my walker and heed every warning.

I do my exercises religiously, fanatically, because I retain the cautionary tale of my mother, who never did her physical therapy unless in the presence of a physical therapist and never really walked again after her hip replacement. I realize I am in much better health and much better equipped for recovery than my mother was at the end of her life, but still. I am not messing around. I perform my regimen three times a day. I become the star pupil at the physical therapy clinic. They give me progressively harder things to do, and I do them awesomely. I almost feel like I can dance again.

My husband, fresh from on-the-job caregiver training with his father, is a master caregiver. He brings a massive vase of flowers to the hospital. All the nurses come to see them. He holds down the fort at home. He buys the unmentionable thing I realize I need at home, which is an adjustable seat over the toilet that keeps me from bending more than ninety degrees when sitting to do my business. He puts a black garbage bag on the seat of the car so that I can slide my bottom easily. He readies the spare room for me, as I can't yet climb the stairs to our bedroom. I think he is secretly relieved not to be sleeping next to me, because he wouldn't sleep a wink if he had to sleep next to someone he views as a fragile piece of the finest china, but he doesn't say this. I know he is worried he will find me fallen or dead in the morning, but he doesn't say this either. He cooks for me. He watches old movies with me. He refreezes my ice pack. He helps me put on socks. Correction: he literally puts my socks on my feet. He drives me to all my appointments. He tells me I'm doing great. He is my biggest cheerleader. He could totally do this for a living.

I ask Nurse Heather if I can go on a four-hour drive to celebrate Thanksgiving at my daughter's house, which is new and she's just moved into, and she says I have to be sure to stop and get out and stretch every two hours. It's just before my six-week recheck with my surgeon. I ask Nurse Heather if I'm okay to have sex. She says I can do whatever I want as long as I don't cross my legs or turn my toes in or bend more than ninety degrees or cause myself any pain. "I don't know how athletic you get, but pain means stop," she says. I can hear her smile over the phone.

I have to stick to low-impact exercise, and I have to take antibiotics before I go to the dentist for the next year because infection can travel quickly from mouth to new hip. I graduate from a walker to a cane, but the cane becomes unnecessary except to fend off my daughter's enthusiastic dogs. I get to go back upstairs to my own bed, snug against my husband, and I only use one foot on each stair instead of two. I feel like a miracle.

At Thanksgiving I can hardly express the depth of my gratitude for my new hip, for my medical providers, for my caregiver, for my family, for Medicare, for my new lease on life. I am surprisingly mobile, almost pain-free, and so grateful to live such a privileged life.

Turn back, my soul, to your rest, for the Lord has been good to you.

—Ps 116:7

Balancing Outrage and Acceptance

So with old age is wisdom, and with length of days understanding.

—Jb 12:12

The nurse who weighs and measures me at a routine medical appointment is trying to say that I have shrunk an inch in height. I think, "Well, thanks for that news, ma'am." I'm finding there's a lot of shrinking going on in my body. I'm pretty sure my brain used to be bigger. My hair used to be thicker. But getting noticeably shorter is something that happens to old people.

When did this oldness occur? I might have officially become an old lady when I started keeping tissues in my pocket. Or maybe it was when I began keeping an eye out for handrails. Or having lascivious thoughts about a grandpa.

Perhaps the most critical aspect to coping with the aging process with any degree of success is to approach the difficulties we face with grace and humor. Outrage is cheap and easy. Acceptance takes a lifetime to cultivate, so we should be better at it than we are.

I attended my paternal grandmother's funeral with my parents. My grandmother was the last of her generation, having outlived all her siblings and their spouses on both sides of our family. At the luncheon my father's cousin, a shriveled little thing, hugged my dad and said, "Buddie! You haven't changed a bit!" This made me smile; he'd obviously changed a *lot* since he and this batty old lady were kids sixty years earlier.

My mother looked at my father with new eyes then and exclaimed, panic in her voice, "We're the old people now!" The realization devastated her. I'd already thought of my parents as the old people, but she had not until that moment.

A T-shirt for sale pops up on my social media that reads, "It's weird being the same age as old people." It is. But you don't have to market it to me.

When I was a (much) younger writer, throwing words together in between bouts of real life with a husband and four children, I dreamt of being able to afford one of those writing retreats advertised in writing magazines: a cabin in the woods or maybe an apartment in Paris, a place where a writer can go to write. There would be solitude stretching from morning to night: no carpools, no lunches to pack, no laundry, no unscheduled trips to the vet, no homework to nag about, no balanced-meal prep, no noses to wipe, no arguments to settle. The only daily task would be to write. How glorious! I knew I would write fantastic things if I could go on a retreat.

Now that I am a (much) older writer, I could probably afford a few weeks away in the woods. Now I have room for leisure. Now, in my empty nest, life is predictable. And now, as I read through the most recent issue of *Poets & Writers*, the ads for retreats and private spaces do not call my name. I have arrived at a place where I pretty much live a retreat-like life every day. How lucky is that? The years of writing while negotiating a house full of kids have given me the ability to write quickly and efficiently in any space, in any noise. While that skill still serves me well, I realize I don't need a retreat to have time to write. How lucky am I?

Yet sometimes I miss the frenzy, the haphazardness, the incessant demands on my person; I miss the sheer cacophony of family against which I'd longed for quiet. Those decades with my darlings all home were fiercely hectic, and yet they provided a mighty flow of raw material for writing. I have written a family-oriented weekly column for a newspaper for over twenty years, and I've freelanced for magazines since the last century. I even wrote a book about marriage, which was a labor of great love, although it was a commercial failure. My writing was never lucrative enough to take the place of a full-time job, but it financed some extra joy around the house. I suppose that was payback for the richness of ideas that my family life generated. I wrote on deadline and on the fly. I always thought I'd be a better writer if only I had the time.

Am I, though?

In my palpably silent house, I sometimes feel as dry as the desert. My children are grown. They have fledged and are navigating their own adventurous skies. I have aged along with them. I am well past the midpoint of my life; my bones have thinned, and my patience has lengthened. I am more reflective and less impulsive. I am more wrinkled and less limber. As the newspaper business has shriveled, my column has been cut to twice a month, and maybe that's a good thing because my ideas are a bit menopausal. Here's the irony of now: I have time, space, and money. I have a fancy laptop. I even have my own office in a bedroom, which used to be decorated in a leopard motif when it housed my youngest daughter and which I have repainted a color called Zen green. But do I have anything to say?

Some days I say no. I say that I am desiccated; I am done. But then something happens—a sound, a gesture, a connection, a reaction, an impression, a tiny synapse, and I get that feeling that writers get, that *I have to get this down*. I have to catch the words coursing through me before they disappear. Sometimes I have to write with such urgency that I can compare it to the urge to throw up. Emitting a rough draft is like vomiting, just getting the roiling ideas out of my system and onto paper or screen. My writing hours fly as I wrestle with a word or clarify a thought or cut a stupid phrase or ponder the direction of an essay.

Then I know I have something to say. Writers write the same way that they breathe—that is, out of necessity. I am a classic introvert, but I have managed to stir up my share of fusses with the written word. I need to write. I love to write. I love to be read. It's just that my raw material has changed along with me. I find I listen more than I opine these days. My need to be the burning center of everything has calmed. Retired from my day job, I can spend whole days writing, from morning to night. Perhaps life as we age becomes one long retreat. Maybe in my dotage, I'll write pertinent things, because writers don't retire; they die. How lucky is that?

We can complain and commiserate about the trials of aging, the outrages of stiffening joints and forgetful brains, but there are cool things about aging as well: we get to learn stuff, the kind of random stuff that we didn't have time for when we were working full-time and raising kids and maintaining a household. My latest obsession, perhaps encouraged by the amount of time the pandemic kept me at home after I'd retired, is pelicans. Specifically, it is the brown pelican, or *pelicanus occidentalis*, which is a term I learned from the internet. The pelicans come to the northern Oregon coast seasonally and stay from April to November. They winter farther north, in British Columbia, which seems odd because human adult old birds go south for the winter. I just know that the pelicans are firmly entrenched over the ocean outside my window by summer. I watch them flying through my spotting scope, which is another thing you may find yourself owning in retirement; they move as though choreographed, doing their dramatic dives.

I've learned that brown pelicans only mate for one season at a time rather than for life, like this human old bird did. One late spring evening, as I was watching the pelicans congregate on the rocks in the ocean, I saw them doing something different. They were deliberately landing in the water and floating gently on the waves before the waves broke. They seemed to be landing and floating in pairs. Then they'd fly off and resettle a short distance way, forming another pair. "Holy cow," I thought, "they're *speed dating*!" I happen to know about speed dating from my oldest daughter, who recently participated in just such a setup at her neighborhood trivia pub. I wondered, What specific qualities are the pelicans checking out in each other? What gives a pelican mating value? Is it a longer neck, a deeper pouch, or just a good sense of humor?

Watching the pelicans fills me with the opposite of outrage, which is a grateful acceptance of the absolute gift of being able to hang out at home without an immediate care in the world, watching pelicans go about their business.

This is love: my husband has made me a box. He took an old cardboard box—I think our dog's flea meds came in it—and drew abstract illustrations on it with colored markers. On it he wrote, "Writer at work." Now that we're retired, he often wanders into the room where I'm typing and starts talking to me, interrupting my bubble of thought. I try to be gracious and respond to him, but he can tell I'm not really tracking the conversation. So he has asked me to set it on the table next to me whenever I'm working so he knows not to bother me. When I look at that box, covered in designs and doodles, I just see so much love. Here is a side note: if you manage to marry a good husband, you'll catch the added benefits of him becoming a good dad and a good grandpa.

As I age, I find it easier to deal with setbacks, to roll with the various punches of life. Because I can look back at a long life, I am less crushed by disappointment when a plan doesn't work out or when something doesn't go my way. I am thinking of the best way to say this to my daughter, who has failed her first attempt to pass the bar exam. Three years of law school and months of intensive studying and preparation have ended in her defeat. I know she will pass on a future attempt; I know she will someday look back and breezily mention the time she didn't pass the bar. I just don't know how to say that without sounding callous or indifferent to her present-tense, very real pain.

I want to tell her that sometimes our screwups turn out to be the best thing that could have happened to us but that we only arrive at that insight with the gift of time and perspective. I want to assure her that everything happens exactly as it should, even the terrible things. I know she has the reservoir of determination to dust herself off and take the exam again, but she needs some days to mourn what could have been. She needs to dwell in a small pit of regret, in the if-only thoughts of a crushing disappointment, before she moves on.

"So I hesitate to tell you this because the last time I gave you some news about your eyes, you wrote a column about me," my optometrist said.

I'd forgotten about that column from fifteen or so years ago, which had to do with the dreaded news of my need for bifocals.

"Tell me anyway," I said.

"You have the tiniest beginning of a cataract in your left eye," he said.

A cataract! Oh, unhappy day. Cataracts are signs of decrepitude. Cataracts happen to my mother-in-law. Cataracts form in the cloudy eyes of my twelve-year-old dog (that's seventy-two in people years). Surely, I am too young for a cataract.

My doctor retrieved the model of the big eye from his desk. He slipped a clear plastic disc from a slot in front of the staring eye. "This is the lens of your eye," he explained, "between the iris and the pupil. When we are young, it is flexible and clear."

I appreciated the "we" reference. Still, I didn't like where this conversation was going. I'd gone into my yearly appointment feeling reasonably middle-aged and was leaving an old woman.

"As we age, the lens becomes brittle and eventually gets discolored. That's a cataract."

The eye glared at me. "It's like when you have a ten-year-old car and you notice that the headlights have gotten fogged over," he said. "Sort of like that. But the lens of your eye can be replaced. It's a fairly easy operation."

"So when do I need surgery?" I asked.

"When it bothers you," he said. "You'll know."

Will I? Or will I just get used to muted and cloudier vision?

I have noticed the tendency of other parts to become brittle and inflexible as we age: Our bones. Our learning curves. Our hearts. We get set in our ways, and we become resistant to change at a time when things are definitely changing. It occurs to me that maybe we develop cataracts on the soul.

The wonder and delight in which we bask when we are children can become jaded as we start to take the miracles of life for granted. The first time we see the ocean or a dragonfly or a skyscraper or an actual cow can be a staggering experience. But can we remember that far back? Then, as teenagers, we go out of our way to be unimpressed by things we once thought magical. Maybe adolescence is the foretelling of soul cataracts.

As we mature, we are obsessed with making our living, making our families, making our way in the world, making our lasting mark. By the time we are old, everything can seem mundane, or disappointing, or permanent. We have suffered setbacks and disillusionment, rejection and failure. We have mourned losses that break our hearts and challenge our faith in a loving God. All of these things can cloud the eyes of our souls. They can lead to spiritual blindness.

How do we break through those spiritual cataracts? What surgery of the soul can restore the clarity of God's love and plans for us? Perhaps we would do well to find new ways to pray, to bring ourselves into a fresh and lucid intimacy with God. Perhaps we can remove the clouded lens of our soul by a conscious attempt to see anew the ways in which God invites us to delight in all creation, the small joys and wonders that surround us every day and that we have not taken the time or the care to notice for years. Perhaps our souls will again become crystal clear if we can see our way to accept changes, to be curious, and to embrace life's surprises.

Cataracts, both physical and spiritual, can be cured. The cool thing, according to my optometrist, is that when the cataract surgery is complete, the patient often no longer needs glasses. For someone who's worn glasses since childhood, this is welcome news. I may be wrinkled and bent by the time I go under the eyeball knife, but my vision will emerge as twenty-twenty.

And what will then become of my brittle soul? Perhaps if I follow my own advice, it, too, may become flexible and transparent again as it allows itself to go with the flow and to go with God.

❖

The caregiving for my dad was especially difficult because he had always been the alpha male of the family. To be so dependent was impossibly hard for him. "Your father's a pain in the neck," he said to me at one point, in a lucid moment. "You're spending your whole weekend here."

"That's what families do," I said. "Good thing we have a big one."

"It's too much," he said.

"You'd do it for me, Dad," I said.

"I did do it for you," he answered.

And there it was: the cycle of child, parent, child—or parent, child, parent. The father of my childhood, who was as tall as the roof of the front porch and as hearty as a lumberjack after a pancake breakfast, who could figure out and triumph over anything life threw at him, was frail, mere skin and bones, weakened by the betrayal of organs and the erosion of years, relying on others to keep all the balls in the air.

One of my daughters visited for a weekend, and when she hugged me goodbye, our embrace lasted much longer than usual. I could feel her strong young body against my tired one, both comforting me and seeking comfort. I thought of how my dad's body felt so terribly fragile against mine when I hugged him now, and I wondered if my body felt more brittle to her. I realized that I might one day be in her and her siblings' capable, loving hands.

I think of my dad saying, "I did do it for you," and I know what he meant. We care for our children with all our heart and strength. They grow up and look their future in the eye, and we think we did pretty well. They watch us age and falter, and they know that they may someday need to take care of us. And so it goes. We know from our elders that aging will eventually take everything from us, including life. But what a ride.

I got my latest email from Medicare: "How to choose a nursing home." Yikes.

I chanced upon a new word today: *labile*. I had to look it up. It's possible that I've looked it up before, that it's one of those words that, no matter how many times I look it up, I do not remember its meaning the next time I see it. (Do we all have a secret list of words we just can't grasp? At the top of my list is the word *sanguine*. I find it impossible to hold on to what that means.) Labile, an adjective, is pronounced with long-A and long-I sounds. It means liable to change, or unstable. It's sometimes used to describe a chemical compound, but I like it as a descriptor of the state of being alive. The older we get, the more we see that life can change in a split second, that everything is tenuous and fragile, that our existence is liable to change. We as people are labile. Our situations are labile. However much we may want things to remain the same, we know they will not. We can waste a lot of time being outraged by this, or we can accept the changing nature of ourselves, our bodies, our minds, our relationships, and our lives.

Is there a corresponding noun, like *lability*? Yes, there is. Lability refers to something that is constantly undergoing change or is likely to undergo change; it comes from the Latin *labilis*, meaning prone to slip. Apparently, emotional lability is a medical thing meaning rapid and uncontrollable changes in mood, which sounds to me like a synonym for perimenopause. But it is existential lability that interests me, especially as a person wrestling with the realities of navigating her mid-sixties. Being labile means that we are one small aneurysm, one rapidly dividing cancer cell, one arterial blockage, or one little fall away from a complete change—or even end—to the life we know.

Do we brood on this, or do we bury it? The balance between outrage and acceptance is like the balance between resentment and gratitude. We can resent the passing of years or be grateful that we are here for them. We can fear the unexpected changes, or we can navigate them with grace. We are labile, but love is not. We are aging, but the world keeps turning.

Every day, millions of puzzle fanatics sharpen their pencils or charge their phones, ready to meet the challenges awaiting them. I am one of them. Each morning, I make a cup of coffee, let the cat out, open my online newspaper subscriptions, and get busy.

I recognize the danger of having so many puzzles to choose from: I could solve puzzles all day and not actually ever get out and live my life—or what's left of it. I try to do the crossword, Wordle, Spelling Bee, and Connections, and that's just the offering of the *New York Times*. I do the Jumble and sudoku from another paper. I do these daily puzzles for my brain. My cousin, who shares the genetic history of dementia and Alzheimer's disease on the side of the family tree that we climb in common, also faithfully pursues his morning regimen of brain games. I suppose all of my cousins on my mother's side, of whom there are many, live with some lurking possibility of the kind of mental death that preceded our parents' physical deaths. Some of us accompanied our mothers or fathers as they lost their struggles with names and faces and memories, then with basic tasks and hygiene and language. Our parents' deaths broke our hearts but fueled a commitment to maintaining healthy brains. My cousin and I don't know if our brain games will save us, but we cling to the science and the hope. And the studies, while not conclusive, are encouraging: the Mayo Clinic notes that if you challenge your brain with puzzles, "you may keep yourself mentally fresher and sharper for a longer period of time. . . . There is increasing evidence now that lifestyle modifications can affect your cognitive function going forward. That doesn't mean that lifestyle modifications will necessarily prevent Alzheimer's disease. . . . However, physical activity is healthy for your body, and playing games is just plain fun."

Yes, plain fun!

My cousin and I know that games are in our family's blood, which was personified by our card-playing grandmother. When she visited us, she'd be dealing me a hand of cards the moment I got home from school, before I'd even taken off my coat and set down my book bag. "I have homework," I'd say, but she always urged me to put it off for just a bit. She'd pull in my older brother and younger sister sometimes as well. She taught us card games that I haven't played in years, like crazy eights and hearts and spades. She also taught us solitaire so that, as long as we had a deck of cards, we'd never be bored. My grandmother was not the type of sweet old grandma who would let the youngest kid win. *Hell no.* She was a cutthroat competitor. She played to win. She wanted to beat the pants off you. If you ever beat her, you'd earned that victory. She also had a passion for board games, with her favorite being Pop-O-Matic Trouble. I can still hear that hard-plastic bubble over the single dice popping. My grandmother died of a fast-moving brain cancer in her midseventies, which was an early and bruising encounter with the death of a loved one for all her grandchildren, of whom, as I've noted, there were many. The brain games did not save her.

Still, she bequeathed us a curiosity about new things—styles and trends and music that we young people were embracing—the kind of active interest in life that also engages the brain. Older folks, and I include my Medicare-eligible self, can become set in our ways; we can be tied to the past, suspicious of the present, and may predict only doom for the future. We can lose our sense of wonder: if unused, our brains can atrophy along with our muscles. Even our puzzle-solving routines can become a mental rut if they shut out the light of a new day. "Lifestyle modification," as the Mayo Clinic delicately puts it, is necessary to aging gracefully. As long as our brains can handle it, we would do well, in addition to the brain games, to take a moment to appreciate the world as it changes around us, to listen to new ideas, to embark on new adventures, even to try a new food. Our future brains may thank us. Our genes may eventually do us in, but we can go down swinging.

For my days vanish like smoke.

—Ps 102:4

CHAPTER 8

In Praise of Invisible Women

For our lifetime is the passing of a shadow.

—Wis 2:5

Aging women face the harsh reality of becoming invisible in our society—in the movies, on television, in the workplace, on the street, and just about everywhere the public eye cares to look. The invisibility cloak that seems to settle over us makes us realize we could totally get away with committing crimes in broad daylight because no one really sees us. Men, famous or not, can pull off looking older and *distinguished*, but women are meant to look seamlessly young. When women, famous or not, try to Botox their way to eternal youth or surgically deny the merciless march of the seasons, their look becomes plastic, unnatural, and sometimes tragic. But when women don't try to hide their wrinkles or their graying hair, they become invisible. We older women try our best to age with grace by embracing our inner crone and accepting the effects of gravity, but there comes a time when we notice that we get called ma'am a lot. We catch sight of ourselves in a mirror and are surprised by the older versions of the women we forgot to expect looking back at us. We do the math and realize that all those handsome firefighters and cops and doctors we encounter are the age of our children (or grandchildren!). We no longer catch a random man's eye lingering on some part of our anatomy, which is something we never thought, when we were younger and more frequently ogled, that we'd miss. The experience of not being treated like a sex object can be liberating. But it can also be secretly disheartening to realize that in the subjective eye of society, we have disappeared.

If you've never had a hot flash, let me describe one for you. You are going about your life in the usual way when something randomly turns up the flame under your central heating system. The temperature in the room or the office or the car or the backyard has not changed, but something in you has. You are abruptly blanketed in a tight heat. You feel like your face has reddened, but as you feel that hotness creeping over your entire body, you wonder, How can your entire body be embarrassed? You are so hot that it's all you can think about for a bit; all your brain can think is that *it's so hot*! Your brain worries it might boil. You can visualize frying an egg on your stomach. You understand how a lobster in a steam pot feels at the moment of death. And then the wave recedes, the grip of heat loosens, and you feel a little clammy, almost a little cold, and more than a little irritated. You resent the hormonal ambush. You are relieved it's over, but you just can't get over how *hot* it was for that minute.

I hope I haven't lost my male readers with that long-winded description, because even though men may think they are not affected by hot flashes, if a man lives with a woman who experiences hot flashes, he may benefit by continuing to read. Yes, that means you, brave husband of a menopausal wife. Try to sympathize: if you were to close yourself in the bathroom, turn the hot faucet in the shower to full blast, crank up a space heater, down a hot toddy, and wrap yourself in a parka, you might get the *hot* part, but you still wouldn't fully understand the instantaneous or unbidden part, the *flash* part. A hot flash is seriously not a fun thing to have happen to you. It is unpleasant, it is draining, and it reverberates through body and soul with the prickly message that you are getting old and you are not in control of yourself. You have ceded control to your hormones, and they are vindictive. You see why your wife seems a little off?

At some point I morphed from an energetic young mother to a confident woman whom you could hear roar to a . . . what? A senior citizen. An old broad. A menopausal crone. Sometimes I catch sight of myself in a mirror, and I don't recognize this prune-ish lady. I feel like I could start at the top of my head and work my way down, resulting in a catalog of what is wrong with each part of me: My hair is turning gray. My eyes need reading glasses. Random hairs sprout coarse and witchlike from my chin. An urban road map lines my neck. My breasts dip to half-mast. My bladder fights the good fight of retention. And so this continues toward the floor, with each body part having issues and failings, right down to ankles that creak in the morning and toes that can no longer manage a night out in high heels. And over it all, there is the hot flash that astonishes me with the merciless way it swoops in anytime, anywhere, and makes me feel dried out.

Are you still reading, husband of a menopausal woman? This is why you should do something unexpectedly sweet once a hot flash has run its course. When I am feeling chaotic and wobbly, I am amazed and grateful that my husband still loves and desires a wreck like me.

I know, things could be worse. I've had a happy life while earning each fine fissure on my face. A wise woman once told me to think of a hot flash as a power surge, a positive spin to make an uncomfortable moment more comfortable. It does, in a way. As we boomers age, and as we dissect our physical realities, we really are empowered by our move out of the closet of decorum.

We don't whisper in the kitchen about our menopausal symptoms; we write books about them. My generation has risen to confront the indignity—and the mythology—of aging. We research the remedies: hormonal replacement therapy (too dangerous?), eliminating caffeine (oh, please—always a terrible idea), and dressing in layers (look out for flying thermals). We try herbal supplements and meditation and online workouts. We count our blessings and work on our attitude. We are delighted to be done with monthly bleeds; we are ready for the challenges ahead—that is, until the next hot flash.

At least hot flashes aren't as regular or as enervating as labor pains. Then again, labor pains produce something tangible and wonderful. Maybe we crones should treat those power surges as the pangs that will birth a liberated woman who is better than ever. If nothing else, we know we're *hot*.

Nora Ephron once wrote about feeling bad about her neck, and I do, too, especially when I see a photo of myself looking down. My mom used to say that no matter how much plastic surgery (or "work," as it's euphemistically termed) an older woman might undergo, the neck, with its freakish scrotal folds, always gives away her real age—unless she makes friends with fashion scarves.

My daughter, an esthetician, informed me that men's necks are less revealing because they shave their necks throughout their adult lives, which acts as an ongoing exfoliant. If only I'd known. Sometimes I'd like to shave the delicate old-lady fur that has cropped up along my upper lip and jawline, but I'm just not that into skin maintenance. If I were, I would have been tweezing and waxing and sunscreening and moisturizing for the past million years. I think I'm too lazy to be well preserved.

We women are supposed to be at war with Mother Nature and Father Time, those parental figures of our temporal downfall. We fight them with Faustian fervor as we spend many millions on the pretense of antiaging. The ridiculously expensive nighttime cream that my esthetician daughter has recommended hilariously claims to arrest age. I assure you no arrests have been made. I slather the potion on anyway, as though to stop would be to surrender to the age authorities, but my neck eludes capture. We applaud (and envy) actresses and models who beat back their actual age with their deceitful appearance. We, too, aspire to pass as younger than we are. We scrutinize the older women on television vying for the prize of the widower known as *The Golden Bachelor* and try to determine who's had what kind of work done on what body part or whose face doesn't move in any discernable way, bless their hearts. We see impossible role models in their seventies, like tiny Dolly Parton prancing in her cheerleader outfit, or even in their eighties, like old Martha Stewart looking pretty sexy on the cover of *Sports Illustrated*, for God's sake, and we can despair. The photos of Martha make her look like she is thirty years younger than she is, but I wonder, Do her limbs have to remember how to walk after a long car ride, like the rest of us seniors? Or has she discovered the fountain of eternal cartilage? I'm sure that no amount of money or makeup or "work" or working out is ever going to qualify me for the cover of the bathing suit issue. I guess I am pretty much okay with that.

I go along with the reality of the aging process with the exception of my hair. I religiously dye it back to the color it was when I was born. I tell myself that this is more matter of identity than vanity: when you are born with red hair, you stand out only because of your hair. Your hair defines you. It is an integral part of who you are and who you are perceived to be. When my hair started lightening itself and a person I'd recently met referred to me as a blonde, my heart nearly stopped: I am not a *blonde*. I am a redhead. I've been a redhead *all my life*. I have the freckly blotchy skin to prove it. My esthetician daughter—bless her!—taught me how to color my hair at home, which is easy on the beauty budget.

She picked out a shade that approximates the color of my youth, and for now, I am sticking with it. Sometimes when that white stripe of new roots starts emerging on top of my head, I consider letting it all go to white. I wrestle with my vanity. I worry that my lying hair is too young for my wrecked face. But I think of St. Augustine when I think about having white hair—about the idea that no one will know I'm a redhead unless they've known me for a long time—and his loosely translated confession: "Oh, Lord, make me good—but not yet!"

In Greek mythology a naiad was one of the water nymphs who presided over brooks, springs, and fountains. In American mythology the marathon swimmer Diana Nyad has presided over many bodies of water. Nyad is her actual last name, acquired from her stepfather.

Diana Nyad is known for her long-distance swimming. She never swam in the Olympics, but she broke time records swimming around the island of Manhattan in 1975, as well as from the Bahamas to Florida in 1979. Over the years, I followed Nyad's decades-long quest to swim from Cuba to Florida. She tried to do so five times, failing the first four times due to storms, impossible currents, multiple jellyfish stings, or trouble with her support boat. In 2013 she finally accomplished her goal. Our American naiad presided over the Florida Straits, the perilous stretch of sea from Cuba to Florida that connects the Gulf of Mexico to the Atlantic Ocean. In about fifty-three hours, she swam 110 miles from Havana to Key West, the first person to do so without the protection of a shark cage. She emerged shaky and salty and depleted, but she did it. She was sixty-four.

At sixty-four, Nyad made our youth-obsessed culture recognize the value of resilience. In our male-dominated culture, she made us believe in the power of womanhood. Along with every marvelous, accomplished woman of a certain age, she reassures us women that we can thrive in our senior years. We are wiser, more centered, more balanced, and more assured in our own skins. We know our limits, but we also know how to stretch ourselves toward our dreams. If we've paid attention to the lessons of life, we've become more forgiving and more compassionate but also more committed. We're more aware of the urgency of each moment. And I believe that as we mature and learn to let go of the flimsy, silly superficialities that preoccupy us in our youth, we become more beautiful. Although society makes us doubt ourselves at times and makes us feel invisible—indeed, teaches us to be invisible—we can believe that we've still got it. It's just that the definition of "it" is a bit deeper and a bit kinder. If we focus, we can see past the mirror to the truth that we've still got the "it" that matters. We have earned the title of age warrior.

On those days when the lighting is harsh, my bones are creaking, I get my senior discount without asking for it, and I feel my advanced age, I hold Diana Nyad in my mind's eye, and I'm good to go. If she can swim to Florida, I can face the day. Because, as she has shown us, it's not so much about the swimming as it is about the heart.

When my husband and I were weighing where to retire, an older friend gave me this advice: "Make sure you both want to live in that house and in that town because one of you will live there alone one day." Her words froze me. Statistically, however, she is right. Barring some freakish accident or spectacular act of God, my husband and I will die at different times, and one of us will be left.

I hate to think of it. Even the potential grief for my husband paralyzes me. Once, another older friend told me that he used to want to be the first to die so as to spare himself the mourning and the loneliness of losing his life partner. But when his wife was diagnosed with Alzheimer's and he was caring for her, he changed his mind. He told me, holding back tears, that now he prayed that she would go first because she wouldn't understand where he'd gone, and no one else would take care of her like he did. I realized that I was in the presence of the personification of holiness and devotion, of true and selfless love.

His wife did indeed die before him.

It's hard to imagine living alone when you've been one-half of a long marriage—to eat alone, sleep alone, travel alone, make decisions alone—but I now have friends doing exactly those things. Some of them are younger than I am. Most of them are women: for every widower I know, I know five widows. I see them fade from view once the funeral is over and everyone they love goes back to their normal lives. I note the signs of shell shock on the faces of my older friends as they navigate their new normal. Some of them are defeated by the many tasks their husbands once took care of, including the way my own mother could not cope with the mechanics of living on her own. She hadn't prepared. She'd been caught off guard, and she was mad at my dad for leaving her in the lurch. She briefly tried living alone in a little guesthouse near one of my sisters, but it became apparent that she would be safer and more closely cared for in an assisted-living facility. In spite of the new neighbors and activities available to her there, I think she spent a lot of each day alone.

Sociologists write about the epidemic of loneliness in our society, with social isolation an increasing phenomenon among older adults. According to the Pew Research Center (www.pewresearch.org), there are 16.7 million Americans over the age of sixty living alone, which is about one in four of us. Women are more likely to live alone than men due to their longer life expectancies and the higher rate of widowhood. The gap widens the older we become.

When I imagine the sobering prospect of being the one left, I think about the prosaic: who will eat the yellow bananas? Who will clean out the rain gutters? Then I think about the poetic: how will I survive on half a heart?

I try not to dwell on the inevitable. I try not to be fatalistic, like wondering if this is the one that will be our last anniversary, or our last Christmas, or our last year together. I try to focus on the blessed familiarity and dependability of my husband's presence, on how much I love and adore him, on the comfort and joy of being together as we age. I know whichever one of us is left will manage to do what is needed. One of us will be a single person, a single parent, and a single grandparent. And it will slam a door in the soul. And seem unbearable.

I think of the widows I know; some are thriving and some are faltering. I don't want to join their ranks anytime soon. But I want them to know as they grieve and go on that they are loved, they are beautiful, and they are not invisible to God.

She is clothed with strength and dignity, and laughs at the days to come.

—Prv 31:25

CHAPTER 9

Circling to Land

Oh that today you would hear his voice: Do not harden your
hearts.

—Ps 95:7–8

In 1998 I wrote a poem about being older, although I was
forty-one. In 1998 I thought that was old. I was flying from Los
Angeles to Washington, DC, to meet my husband, who was about
to complete a bike ride across America. The bike ride, a charitable
fundraising event, had lasted almost six weeks. I was seated next to
a young woman on the plane who seemed like everything that I, a
tired mother of four, was not—or, more accurately, was no longer.

The plane had to circle for a while, awaiting a gate opening
for us to disembark. My thoughts on our circling turned into this
poem. Now in my midsixties, I feel the metaphor of circling right
down in my bones.

Circling

The girl next to me on the plane
reminds me of myself

twenty years ago.
On the red-eye flight,
she orders hot tea
⠀⠀⠀—she asks for lemon—
she reads "War and Peace"
⠀⠀⠀—her bookmark,
⠀⠀⠀⠀⠀a jaunty third of the way through—
she's a college grad
who wears tiny dark-rimmed glasses
and a thrift-shop blouse
with her Levis and Jesus sandals.
She writes a card
⠀⠀⠀in Medieval monk printing
to a boy
who is a friend-not-her-boyfriend.
He lives in England.

I lean sleepy by the window
in my new white sneakers
thinking about my husband
⠀⠀⠀—to whom I'm flying—
wishing for his hands and company.
I furtively devour her card,
without benefit of the reading glasses I will need
⠀⠀⠀next year.
"How goes it, *cher*?
I am on a plane to Detroit, Michigan,
of all places, going to
my oldest friend's WEDDING. As Tolstoy says . . ."

Just wait, I think at her meanly.
(No, don't be mean.)
Just wait, I amend to a wise crone thought.
They'll come your way:

joys, sorrows, countless cards to friends,
    poems, a thousand cups of tea,
    novels thick and thin.
Your writing will get roomier,
and you may get contact lenses.
Your own daughter will begin to make
    her As and 7s funny.
Then you will meet yourself
    —in serviceable shoes—
on a plane
circling to land.

One can see why my career as a poet never took off.

But I still remember so clearly the sense I had on that flight of the way we pass from one generation to another without our noticing, the way we become our elders in the seeming blink of an eye. When I wrote that poem, my own kids were in the throes of their teenage years, and their angsty episodes forced memories of my own chaotic teenage years. But the way they stormed on, insisting that I could not possibly have any idea of what their lives were like, any clue of what they were experiencing, had been assuring me all summer that I really was the adult in the room, even if I sometimes doubted it. I remember at one low point in my self-esteem, I called a friend from college, asking him to tell me that I had once been cool.

"You were cool. You were the coolest," he said. "Don't let those kids make you think you weren't."

It was enough, that sweet voice from my past. I'd been cool, but now I was the mom in my serviceable shoes, clambering to a higher branch of the family tree.

The story of Hannah in the first book of Samuel always tears my heart a little when I hear it. Hannah is childless and is almost past hoping for a child. Yet she persists in praying for a baby. Her prayer is answered, and she becomes pregnant. She promises to repay God for the favor. The price of having the baby, though, is handing the child over to the service of God. She has the baby only to lose the baby.

The idea of having to pay God back for a prayer granted has always bothered me: how can we ever sufficiently pay back grace that is freely given? Even more personally distressing than that, though, is the scene where Hannah brings her weaned son, Samuel, back to the temple where she prayed for his conception and leaves him there. "For this child I prayed," says Hannah, "and the Lord has granted me the petition that I made to him. Therefore, I have lent him to the Lord; as long as he lives, he is given to the Lord" (1 Sm 1:27–28). At that time, Jewish children were nursed for the first two years of life, so I try to imagine carting my two-year-old to church and leaving her there for someone else to love and teach and raise. I know the honor of giving one's child to the service of God is supposed to be enough for a mother, but I don't know that I could have borne the pain of separation that accompanied the honor.

And yet the time always comes when we do give our children to God. Raising a child to adulthood is a series of surrenders because trusting that your parenting has gone well is the only way to allow your child to mature to young adulthood. The first day of school, the first time alone at home, the first signs of physical maturity, the driver's license, the series of graduations—these are all times of handing over our children to God. We cannot always be the guiding force in our child's life, much as we may want to be. We have to allow other teachers, other influences, and other experiences to take hold. We have to trust God and let go. Hannah's letting go of her darling happens at far too young an age for me to contemplate, but we are never really ready for the letting go. It always comes faster than we expect.

Letting go is often against our will. We have to uncurl our fingers consciously. We have raised life warriors. We have to extend our empty arms, wish our loved ones well, and send them on their holy way.

In his apostolic exhortation *Amoris Laetitia*, or *The Joy of Love*, Pope Francis writes that the sacrament of marriage "involves a series of obligations born of love itself, a love so serious and generous that it is ready to face any risk" (sec. 131). After over four decades of marriage, I get that. My husband and I have seriously and generously faced all sorts of obligations and risks that have challenged and graced us, broken and bonded us. We have even just weathered the riskiness of a whole year of looking only at each other's faces during a global pandemic, and we still like each other.

I was thinking recently about the phrase in Genesis about two becoming "one flesh" (Gn 2:24). It was sunset, and our two fleshes had just made one. Sunset has become my favorite time to make love because it is an apt metaphor for this late chapter of our lives—and because its soft light flatters my flesh. It is also especially sweet because, during much of our marriage, sunset was never a time for lovemaking, what with four children and activities and jobs and homework and chores and dinnertime and all the rest of it. Love at sunset might have happened on the rare vacation without the kids, but it was otherwise an impossible dream.

During our childbearing years, we tried to be good Catholics when we had sex. We charted my cycles to space the births of our children. A few times, we sweated out pregnancy scares that turned out to be menstrual lateness. We weren't perfect, as there were definitely occasions when we joined the large percentage of

Catholics who have used other methods of contraception at some point in their lives (see the previous mention of rare vacations, the timing of which could conflict with ovulation). But we tried our Catholic best, taking as our guide the unitive and procreative aspects of married sex that the Church teaches as inseparable. We tended our marriage like a newly planted garden. We were patient and kind, mostly. We were each other's loudest cheerleaders. We were a united parental front. We had plenty of trouble and sacrifice, but we stayed lovers and friends. We still are.

Now our nest is empty of its baby birds, and we enjoy this crazy liberty to do whatever we want, whenever we want. Because we are done making babies, we get to indulge in the unitive part of sex without worrying about the procreative. After the years of policing ourselves, this is a bonus. We may not hear any talk about it from the Sunday pulpit, but we are free to make love at sunset, at sunrise, at noon, at night. Sex with someone you know and love is deeply satisfying. At our age it may involve more careful positioning and lubricative aids. It is probably not as athletic or frequent or spontaneous as when we were young. Still, it is fulfilling. It is affirming. And it is fun.

Marriage can seem like the consolation sacrament, the one you can fall back on when you discern that you do not have a vocation to religious life or the priesthood. It can seem, to married people, that the Church treats sex as an ambivalent duty rather than a sublime gift. *Amoris Laetitia* does its valiant part to elevate marriage to a holy calling. It also assures us of God's joyful love for us, even if our marriages and families aren't traditionally configured. It prioritizes the need for mercy and tenderness in our marriages. And it makes us feel that even if we aren't impeccably behaved, there is hope for us.

I confess I now feel foolish when I remember how bound up in the rules of sex we were when we were young, how we parsed and fretted over the official guidelines, and how we sometimes felt guilty for giving in to passion. The procreative portion of sex commanded a lot more attention than the unitive. Like many married people, we eventually found it more real-life to follow our private, imperfect path. Sometimes we ignored the rules, like the extensive and exhaustive ones about how male orgasm should only happen inside a vagina. (Women's orgasms seem to fly under the radar, which is no surprise. But I digress.) Honestly, it can be a little tiring to read what another celibate person has to say about the "nuptial mystery," to use Catholicism's delicate, not to mention rather lovely, term for sex. With all due humility and respect, I propose that we long-married folks, with a little nudge from the Holy Spirit, might be the grounded experts at unraveling our own unique and blessed nuptial mysteries.

My postmenopausal brain also wonders, If old or infertile couples are permitted the pleasure of unitive sex, why couldn't all couples in good conscience exercise that option? Would that not be in keeping with "the experience of belonging completely to another person" (sec. 319), to refer to *Amoris Laetitia* again? I await the contemplations of the theologians among us.

At sunset the love we send out into the universe comes back to us and folds us into its warmth. In the twilight afterglow, I imagine writing down the recipe for a solid chance at the holy ideal of an indissoluble marriage: God. Love. Trust. Romance. Kindness. Kids. A sense of humor. A reliable vacuum cleaner. Sex at sunset. With these ingredients, two people may find themselves traveling from some fancy vows at an altar to a marriage bed at sunset, with all their hopes and scars and sacred memories to keep them company.

Southern California is lovely in the spring. The hills are green and swooshed with wildflowers, thanks to the epic rains of this past winter. The air is not yet furnace hot, the birds are atwitter, and it seems possible that the wonder of God's creation can coexist with human constructs. But I am here for a specific reason.

Actually, it is for a pair of reasons: my adorable, feisty granddaughter is turning one, and my adorable, feisty uncle is turning ninety. There are two birthday parties a week apart for our extended family to celebrate these loved ones, who are at each end of our time line.

My uncle is the last of the generation that precedes mine on my mother's side. The widower of my mother's sister, he is a godfather and a grandfather and a great-grandfather, and he holds all that we can still know about our family's past. For me, he is the oldest living relative who knew my parents in their salad days. His memories are a treasure.

It is a gift of God, of genes, or of circumstance to live a life of nine decades and counting. My uncle has touched many of our lives in many ways, and it's delightful to see him so appreciated. His children have invited what my mom would have called the immediate world, and many of the same people are attending both parties. First, our family gets to applaud a long life well lived. Then we'll celebrate my granddaughter's brand-new life, brimming with perfect potential. Young and old—both gifts from God.

When I go shopping for birthday cards, I find an entire wall of prospects with a first-birthday theme, with big number ones in riotous fonts flying off the fronts. Then I get to the options for specific decades. For a ninetieth birthday, there are exactly two choices. For one hundred, there is a single lonely offering. Capitalism favors the young.

But life, brand new or long lasting, is what we honor and cherish on these two special occasions. A birthday is a renewal of our faith in everything good. If we believe in God, we trust that our earthly life is just the beginning of our existence, that we will indeed rise. I am mindful that on every Ash Wednesday, our family has been anointed with ashes and told to remember that we are dust and to dust we shall return. But that is too somber a sentiment to mark the space between these two happy birthdays. Instead, I focus on the joy of these holy milestones: my uncle's longevity and my granddaughter's first steps.

Old age is a gift not given to everyone, and we sometimes forget to be grateful for the scores of candles on our cake. And the big number-one birthday candle flickers with our prayer for many moments of grace ahead: a baby is a sign that God wants our human history to keep going. As I enjoy the birthday parties, I'll know that God walks with both of my loved ones, matching an uncle's slow gait and a granddaughter's headlong run, just as I know God walks with each one of us, wherever we are on our journey home.

Our marriage has included the coming and going of seven pet dogs. Our last dog accompanied us into old age. "Think of him as a ninety-year-old man," the vet said on one of our last visits. His walks got very short at the end because a ninety-year-old man (like my uncle) couldn't be expected to navigate a steep driveway or to keep up the pace of his younger self. He ate little. He slept a lot. He was slow to change positions. He was grumpy. He required pain medication. Then he was gone, off to dog heaven, and I miss him still.

Our morning walk used to go from our front door into the woods beyond our house. I feel like I'm walking with a ghost now when I retrace our old path. In his younger days, I kept him on the leash for the walk away from the house and then let him run as fast as he wanted back home. But I never let him off the leash until we could see the house at the end of the path. "Wait till we can see the house," I used to tell him when he tugged on the leash, straining to be set free. As long as I could see the house, I felt like he'd be safe running loose.

This makes no sense. Just because we could see the house didn't mean that any lurking danger in the woods would leave him alone. He could still be eaten by a coyote or hit by a car speeding up the driveway. For no good reason, I just felt safe when the house was in sight.

This is the same thing I used to say to my little kids when they went outside to play: "Just make sure you can see the house." When I was a young mother, this seemed like sound advice. Now I wonder what I was thinking because, in those days, we lived on two acres on top of a mountain where there were bobcats and rattlesnakes and, once, even a rumored sighting of a mountain lion. My kids would go out to play, climbing on giant rocks and conducting puppet shows and building forts, and I somehow thought that as long as they could see the house, they'd be safe. Was I out of my mind? They didn't even have cell phones! I think this is another reason why I was lucky to have my children when I was young: I wasn't worried about the terrible things that can happen to a kid who is outside, playing on a mountain. My kids survived my irresponsible parenting, but you can bet I would not let my grandkids go out to play on snake-infested, bobcat-ridden rocks.

Still, at this late age, being able to see the house is comforting to me whenever I am outside. The house is safety, is comfort, is home. I am tempted to belabor the metaphor of making sure we're able to see the house of God as we venture into the final stages of our lives. But I'll spare you, dear reader. Chances are it's already in your head anyway.

Like a drop of water from the sea and a grain of sand, so are these few years among the days of eternity.

—Sir 18:10

Chapter 10

Generativity and Integrity

God is in heaven and you are on earth; therefore let your words be few.

—Eccl 5:2

The final two of Erik Erikson's eight psychosocial stages of human development are generativity vs. stagnation and integrity vs. despair. Old age happens in the transition between the two. Generativity and integrity shape how we affect the future positively even as we seem to fade from present relevance. Aging strips us down to our framing, to the two-by-fours of who we are and what legacy we leave.

Erickson gives us more existential hope than Shakespeare, whose seventh stage of man reduces us to the bleak image of "second childishness and mere oblivion" at the end of life (*As You Like It*, II, v, 165). With Erickson's insight, we can direct ourselves positively or negatively, depending on our recognition of our deepest selves.

My daughter gave my husband a journal with a title I like: *Slow Noticing*. The unlined pages suggest topics to reflect on or draw. My husband is artistic—unlike me—so it's a thoughtful gift for him: my slow noticing occurs all with words, preferably lined. But I like the long *o* sounds of the title. To notice slowly is to take the time to be observant of a breakneck-speed world, to sort out what matters from what is extra fluff, to hold on to the perfect vision of your heart. But as much as I like the idea and the sound of slow noticing, I am not so crazy about slowing down.

This is because personal speed is not part of aging. We cede speed to the young. I watch my little granddaughter careening around the house, bouncing off bushes in the yard, colliding with the equally enthusiastic dog, and I marvel at her elasticity. The recklessness with which we once moved changes to deliberate steps. Our muscles don't respond as instantly as in the past. We learn to be wary of falling. We slow down for survival. But we don't really like it.

In spite of my current endeavor, I am resistant to writing about aging. This book is a labor of love, but it is hard labor. I am resistant to actually aging. It's as if I believe that if I write about it, my aging becomes more real. This is nonsensical, but it is rooted in me. I am one of those people who is surprised by the old crone they see in the mirror. My reflection is not what I expect, because I picture myself as more vibrant than my actual body's witness. The mirror feels like a betrayal, but it is just dispassionate glass.

I am not alone. Among the friends and family members of a certain age whom I've informally polled, there is a frequent lament that the face and body in the mirror is an ongoing shock, if a shock can be ongoing. Age has given us a common language for reflecting on the losses we've suffered and the lessons we've learned. But my poll has revealed something else I resist, which is a general crankiness about the body aches, the slowed reactions, and the diminished mental capabilities. "I am now a grumpy old man," says one friend. "Though I have avoided ordering people off my lawn, I have descended into a grouchiness that annoys me when encountering change," says another. We sometimes blur the difference between growing old and being old. And we share the sadly standard grievances about the young people: the young people are off the rails, out of control, disregarding society, destroying norms, and so forth—as though our grandparents didn't say the exact same things about us. We see our grandparents in us, we channel them, but sometimes we are unable to control their mouths.

I found a perfect illustration of the divergence of paths in Erickson's seventh developmental stage of generativity vs. stagnation in some news about birds. The American Ornithological Society (AOS) has decided, as of 2024, to reconsider all the English names of birds that presently include a person's surname. The AOS wants to eliminate bird names that may unwittingly honor historical proponents of such social affronts as slavery, racism, or misogyny because these namesakes can be exclusionary, offensive, and painful to bird-watchers in the present tense. The renaming of these eponyms will begin with seventy to eighty birds in the United States and Canada.

I am now wondering about the Steller's jays of the Pacific Northwest. They are showy blue- and black-crested birds whose squawk implies an attitude, and they nest aggressively in the trees outside my house. I thought of them when I read the AOS report and felt prompted to look up Steller, whom I assumed was a man. Of course he was: Georg Wilhelm Steller (1709–1746) was a German explorer in the employ of Russian expeditions. Remembered for his botanical research in the territory of Alaska, his identification of the bird named for him as a relative of the North American blue jay provided evidence that Alaska was indeed part of North America.

Good for Herr Steller. But as the AOS notes in its collective wisdom, the birds named for their "discoverers" existed in places already inhabited by others. They already had names. The birds currently identified by human names, like my friends the Steller's jays, will be renamed for their physical characteristics, bringing attention to the unique beauty of the birds themselves. The AOS hopes that the renaming process, by addressing past wrongs, will engage more people in the enjoyment and protection of birds everywhere.

The perfect illustration of Erickson's seventh stage follows. An older person disposed toward generativity might see the AOS decision as appropriately corrective, an enlightened step forward: progress that is inclusive is a worthy goal. An older person leaning toward stagnation might disparage the AOS decision as ridiculous, as overly and needlessly woke: why can't they leave well enough alone?

Sometimes we older folks need to check our instinctive reactions against the insight of Erickson's stages. It is more helpful to be generative than stagnant. It is more helpful to behave with integrity than despair.

I may not live to see the Steller's jay's rechristening. But I applaud the thoughtful evolution of the AOS. I also hope the new name for my noisy neighbors is easier to say.

My dad said his prayers every night, even when he wasn't sure there was a God. He'd had a serious heart attack in his forties, and after that, he stopped going to church with us. He'd been a lector when I was a kid, so this was a jarring change. "The older I get," he once told me while driving me to the airport to go back to college, "the more I think six feet under is six feet under." I had plenty to ponder on my flight back to a Catholic university.

My dad rejected his Catholicism as decisively as I was embracing mine. Over the years we had discussions about religion and God, even as his heart was failing for good. On the day he died, my dad turned down the opportunity for confession. A priest friend anointed him while he drifted away from us, and I prayed to God to enfold my doubting dad.

Still, he always said those nightly prayers. He couldn't explain why.

But some old letters expressing my young father's faith have helped me understand. After my folks died, my sister held on to a bin of random letters that my parents had written to each other before they were married. When I retired, I offered to organize them by date and transcribe them for the rest of the family. It's been a bigger task than I expected but also a blessing.

The letters date from 1948, when my dad joined the U.S. Navy after graduating from high school. He became a signalman on a destroyer that mainly patrolled the Mediterranean Sea. He wrote letters to a girl he liked back home in New Jersey. She was still a high school senior. He wrote her a lot of letters because she wrote back. She was pretty and funny and had beautiful penmanship.

As I began to type the letters, I felt as though I were meeting these two teenagers for the first time. I fell into the lingo of their youth. Sometimes I'd come away from my laptop feeling like I'd time traveled. I'd blink to get back to my century. The letters contained references to friends I didn't recognize, and I had no one to ask for more information: everyone from that time was gone. I typed my way through to 1949.

My dad wrote the following after shore leave in Italy on Palm Sunday:

> I went to church yesterday in Leghorn, [Livorno] beings it was Palm Sunday and for a change, I enjoyed myself. See if you can picture this, five of us went to a church that had been hit heavy by bombs during the war and has been only partly repaired.

There were about forty other Italians in the church and about twenty kids. Well, I got the idea of giving these people something to remember us by, so we bought all of the Palm that an old lady was selling in the vestibule and passed it out to all of the children and grownups. They appreciated it very much because the people looked at us several times during the sermon as if the priest was speaking of us, even though none of us could understand Italian.

I can picture it.

He described an audience at the Vatican with Pope Pius XII:

While we were in Naples I took a three-day tour to Rome, which cost twenty-three dollars, but this was well worth it because it included all meals and transportation and a very nice hotel room. While in Rome we visited such places as the Coliseum, the Vatican Art Galleries, St. Peter's and St. Paul's churches, the Catacombs, Pantheon, and most important of all we had an audience with the pope himself. There were about thirty in our group and we each had a chance to speak with the pope personally, something that not very many people have ever done or will ever do in their life. Even though I do not consider myself religious, it struck me very deeply to see this great man and is something that I will not forget in a hurry.

I would love to know what my dad and the pope talked about. I do remember family lore about another sailor at the papal audience shouting, "Three cheers for the pope!" followed by a lusty "Hip, hip, hooray!" triad of male responses. The Americans discombobulated the curia present, but my dad said the pope liked it.

My dad wrote pretty introspective letters for a not-quite-nineteen-year-old:

There is one thing though that I have to admit, I've changed in these past few months. I don't know when I first noticed it, maybe it was on a stormy night on the bridge with the rain beating down heavy but not quite leaking through our foul weather jackets or maybe it was on a sunny afternoon when I was sending out a message by flashing lights or perhaps it was when I was sitting in a club in Tripoli, Greece, or Italy. It is not mainly a physical change, although it is a little bit, but a mental one. You begin to think plainer and what you might call "a little more grown up." You don't take anything for granted anymore, especially in Religion. I am getting awfully bad when it comes to going to church. When I think that I didn't go to Mass, Christmas, New Year's, or this morning, I can't help feeling a little low, but if I am home on a weekend, I will have to go to Mass on a Sunday with you, that is if it is all right with you. That is another thing I will be looking forward to besides our date.

My dad managed to get leave in June, in time to take my mom to her senior prom and attend her high school graduation and officially declare his love. The letters get mushy after that. The rest is history: a fifty-eight-years-long marriage, six kids, and sixteen grandchildren.

These glimpses of my dad's long-ago Catholic experiences touched my heart. As he said, he wasn't religious, but he was a thinker. He was plainspoken, irreverent, quizzical, and, in his own way, faithful. We have the letters to prove it. But really, even stronger proof rests in the legacy of his unconditional love.

I was the first of my siblings to make my father a grandfather. My husband and I first announced our coming child at an anniversary dinner for my parents. Throughout the rest of the dinner, my dad kept looking over at me and then shaking his head, saying, "Nah!" with a look of disbelief. He was, at the time, about fifty and probably suffering the tremors of midlife crisis; he wasn't ready to be called Grandpa by anyone. When my sister-in-law repeatedly called him Grandpa that night, my dad was not amused.

Fortunately, pregnancy lasts long enough to give everyone involved the time to adjust to the new roles to be played in the life of the newborn babe. As my physique changed and I became visibly pregnant, my dad's attitude softened. He was genuinely concerned for my well-being and comfort and especially worried on my behalf about enduring labor and birth—never mind that my mom had come through the same experience six times. On the day we brought our daughter home from the hospital, my dad fully embraced his part in her life. It was New Year's Day, and I mentioned that I should have gotten a pacifier for her because it had calmed her in the hospital. The words were barely out of my mouth when my dad was in the car, searching for a store that was open. He returned home with a full bag of supplies: baby wipes, diaper pins, ointments, rattles, a pack of tiny shirts, and several styles of pacifiers. He was an instant doting grandparent and wanted to hold her whenever possible. His initial doubt—his "Nah!"—had been transformed into a loving, joyful "Yes sirree!" During my first difficult days as a new mother, especially when my husband had to return to work, my dad spent many minutes walking with his granddaughter held close, tenderly singing an off-key rendition of "Unchained Melody." Her brand-new life prompted him to say a phrase he would employ repeatedly to his children over the years, referring to the growing number of his grandchildren: "This is what it's all about."

My dad taught me, as well as reminded me with the advent of each of my four children, that every baby is a light, a blessing of possibility, to parents and grandparents, to the whole family. Every baby's birth is a small mirror of the hope and joy brought to the world by the birth of Jesus. We know how much we are loved because a father could send us no greater gift than his son. This is, indeed, what it's all about.

❧

I'm walking on the beach, and I see an old man ahead in my path. He's just standing there. He's looking at the waves, and he's looking at me, and I think, "Oh no, creepy old man." I tense up. I may be an old lady myself, but some men still do and say inappropriate things to old ladies. I'm ready for war, ready to counter whatever appalling thing he's going to say or do.

But as I pass him, he points to the sand and says, "See that sand dollar?"

I see it. It's a whole sand dollar, unusual amid the broken bits of shells that usually wash up out of our rough ocean waters.

"I planted that. For my granddaughter," he says. "She's coming down the beach now with her dad. I want her to find it."

"Got it," I say. It's good he tells me that, or I probably would pick it up. I wish him well and keep walking, but I do so slowly so I can keep turning around to watch this three-year-old little girl reach her grandfather on the shore. I watch her dance around and goof around and then suddenly freeze when she notices the treasure. She picks it up and twirls with it, so excited. She shows her dad and grandpa. They are suitably amazed.

And I am so grateful I got to observe such love in action among these three strangers.

Old men are not always what they seem.

❧

The fact that we can make babies is insanely magical and utterly mundane at the same time. Every species procreates in its particular way in order to sustain its existence and propel it into the future: I like that the reference to sex education as teaching about the birds and the bees is both literal and metaphorical. They—and we—all do it, as the inimitable Cole Porter reminds us. Maybe the way humans reproduce seems miraculous because we have the mental capacity to think about it, choose it, and rhapsodize about it.

Motherhood is a gift I treasure. Today I miss my mother, just as I have every Mother's Day since she died six years ago. But this year, I miss her especially much because my daughter is pregnant with a baby girl. I have so many questions that I didn't know I wanted to ask my mother when she was alive. Now in the grandmother position myself, I wish I could ask her: Did you worry this much when I was pregnant? Did you worry about your daughter suffering complications or (God forbid) death in childbirth the way I do? As one friend said to me when describing grandparenting, did you feel the red-hot DNA from the generations before you projecting through you to the generations after you? Did you feel yourself settling onto an upper branch of the family tree that is so high up it makes you dizzy to look down and where you never imagined yourself perched?

If my mother had any of these thoughts, she didn't ever let on. I'm sure she worried secretly in her heart, but she never voiced any of it. Actually, she might well now tell me that I think too much. My mother was not one for introspection.

But I do remember the one indelible time my mother gently rubbed the infant belly of one of my daughters and said how amazing it was that her tiny ovaries already contained the eggs that would someday ripen and mature into babies, just as this little one had from my ovaries, just as I had from my mother's ovaries, just as she had from her mother's ovaries, and so on, back through the ages. I remember the naked reverence of that moment for both of us. The birth of a child brings out the poet in us, or maybe it's the philosopher within. Birthing a new baby is wild to think about, and it's unremarkably normal at the same time.

I look forward to my daughter's adventure into motherhood as I get to spend her first Mother's Day with her. I consult my memories of being the first-time mother—some are dim; others, vibrant. When you're a mother who's new to the trenches of motherhood, leaking breast milk, wiping a wee behind, and longing for a shower, let alone an adult conversation, you can feel a little resentful of some old crone telling you to cherish these days, that they are fleeting, and that one day, you will miss this time of infancy. "Sure," you think. "You come deal with this load of wash and this grubby floor and these clinging hands." You know motherhood is wondrous, you know you're grateful for the miracle of life—but maybe not just at that exact moment. And the old crone senses your irritation. But let this old crone remind you that Mother's Day is that blessed annual event when maybe you get to sit back and relax, to claim credit for your achievement, and to enjoy your breakfast in bed and your dyed-macaroni-shell necklace.

This Mother's Day feels like a changing of the guard for me. Another mother is having another daughter, a lovely sign of hope for our family and for the world. I am so proud of my daughter and her mothering instincts as she prepares to take her place among parents. It's a daunting task. It's a simple task. It's the most amazing, frustrating, joyful, beautiful, humbling, gratifying, sacred role I've ever played in my life—as I'm certain it will be for her.

I sense my mother's presence especially this Mother's Day. She would have loved being a great-grandma. She loved all babies with a mother's love, and I feel her spirit hovering around her loved ones these expectant days. Her lullabies linger in my heart. The cycle of mother-daughter-mother turns even without her physical presence. The birds and bees do it. Families do it. We'll be falling in love with our newest member. And still the world, oblivious to our blissfulness, keeps spinning.

Jury duty in my small county, as I've learned the hard way, lasts for a whole month. Even if you are on a jury for a week, you still have to call in for the remaining three weeks.

"Are you kidding?" asked a fellow juror after we'd served for several days and reached our verdict. "Aren't we done?"

"We have a smaller population pool to pull from," explained the jury coordinator, who I'm sure had absolutely no power to change the procedures she had to enforce. She paused for emphasis. "This isn't *Multnomah County.*"

No, it isn't. It also isn't Los Angeles County, that enormous lake of prospective jurors from which I'd relocated two years ago. Multnomah County encompasses Portland, the big city to the east of the northern coast of Oregon, and I now live in a much less densely populated county known for its cheese: Tillamook. The name of the high school football team is the Cheesemakers. That's a true story.

So I, now known as Juror no. 40, had obeyed the summons. I believe that jury duty is a special gift that we retired folks can offer our communities. Our system of justice relies on the active and thoughtful participation of citizens like us, and we have time to spare. I also believe that the well-worn joke about the only people serving on juries are the people not smart enough to get out of jury duty is a harmful one. The right to a jury of one's peers, enshrined in the US Constitution, can only come to pass if one's peers actually show up to serve their time in the box. Naturally, there are people who cannot afford to devote any extended time to jury duty: breastfeeding mothers immediately come to mind, as well as the self-employed. Someone in my jury pool told the judge that if they were to serve, the local weekly paper would not make its publication deadline. Either they exaggerated, or they offered literal witness to the sad decline of the newspaper business. The judge excused that juror.

Laws vary by state (and county), but jury duty can be postponed in most jurisdictions: I had postponed mine from June, when I had travel plans, to December. A teacher in the group had also postponed to December, having been under the impression that not a lot of trials were held in the months of winter holidays. The judge contradicted this, however, by noting that so many trials had been delayed because of the pandemic that the December docket was full this year.

So we jurors served. Because of COVID-19 protocols, we could not sit together in the twelve-person box. Instead, we were spread out around the courtroom. This threw the attorneys for a loop: how do you address a jury effectively when some of them are sitting behind you? We could not be excused to the jury room because it was too small to maintain a six-foot social distance among us; every time the judge called a recess, we trooped upstairs to a conference room. Everyone was masked except for when a witness was actually testifying; a mask would make reading facial expressions difficult. Hand sanitizer was stationed everywhere, as its use was required.

Although I called in faithfully each evening for instructions, I only served on one jury. But that was enough to show me the hidden power of jury duty to heal us as a society. Here we were, a group of twelve Americans with nothing else in common other than answering a summons from the government. We'd gotten to know a little about each other when the judge and attorneys questioned us, probing for biases, probably giving us enough information to form opinions about one other. We were of diverse ages, occupations, genders, and ethnicities, and were probably of different religions and political affiliations. We might not have met or conversed with each other anywhere else in the course of our daily lives. But we were tasked with putting all of that aside, as our instructions were to consider only the facts that had been presented in court.

As we deliberated the outcome of a domestic violence case, there was a purity of purpose in the room, an unspoken agreement to do our best to reach a fair verdict on each count. We discussed the law, held preliminary votes, brought up different points we had jotted in our courtroom notes, consulted and pored over the evidence, and listened to each other with respect and careful consideration.

Respect and careful consideration—that's when it hit me: where else would we have listened to each other this way? It would not happen online these days. Not at a school board meeting. Not at a political debate. Not at a family gathering. Not even in church. Our society has become so splintered that I don't know if a random group consisting of such folks as a delivery driver, a nurse, a security guard, a writer, a retired engineer, a teacher, a brewer, and an at-home mom might have been able to engage in a civil conversation anywhere else but in that conference room. That sounds sad. But it seems true.

We have largely partitioned ourselves off from knowing or associating with people with whom we disagree or have nothing in common. I'm reminded of St. Paul's frustration with factions in the early church: "I mean that each of you is saying 'I belong to Paul,' or 'I belong to Apollos,' or 'I belong to Cephas,' or 'I belong to Christ'" (1 Cor 1:12). We belong to our groups just as narrowly. We go to certain parishes, read certain newspapers, visit certain online sites, gather with certain friends, and dismiss everyone and everything we disagree with: we don't want to hear it. We make no room for differences of philosophy or opinion. Our tolerance for debate is at an all-time low. Mostly, we are at war.

At least, I know I am. I'm guilty as charged of the above offenses. But being stuck in a conference room with eleven other jurors has restored my faith in the possibility of any group ever working together again. By the time we reached our verdicts, I felt close to these folks. We'd done our job. I felt a togetherness of commitment, a sense of duty fulfilled, a mutual faith in our imperfect justice system. I admit it: I felt a shared *patriotism* with these strangers. Now I feel refreshed and even hopeful for our country. The system is as good as the commitment we offer it.

I come from a long line of Irish grudge holders, which I have hesitated to write about lest I manifest this miserable quality in my own life. But the joke is on me because it seems the family curse is going to outlive me.

My mother and her six siblings were often at odds with each other, which usually came down to a proclamation that sounded something like "A is not speaking to B." (Names are excised not so much to protect the innocent as to ward off yet another rift in the family.) This problem had to be acknowledged at family events—for example, if A and B were not speaking, then A and C could not be seated at the same table as B and D at a wedding. Feuding siblings skipped weddings and birthdays, christenings and graduations, and anniversaries and funerals when they were not speaking to each other. They lost precious time with each other for seemingly silly reasons. Sometimes siblings eventually made up and mended their differences—if they could even remember what the original fight was about. Just kidding! *Of course* they remembered, and they never ever forgot. This was part of the curse.

When we were young, my five siblings and I thought the aunts and uncles and their various spats were ridiculous. We used to joke about them, these unreasonable relatives of ours. We were never going to be like them. What could ever be serious enough to make you not speak to your brother or sister?

The curse lives on in a too-obvious plot twist: two of my siblings pretty much haven't spoken to me since before my mother died. We barely acknowledged each other at our mother's funeral. "How good and how pleasant it is, when brothers dwell together as one!" gushes the psalmist (Ps 133:1), who definitely never met my family.

And here we are. These two have cut off relations not only with me but with the remaining four of us. We've been unable to resolve our differences, because our accounts of the events that caused the falling-out are radically divergent. I'm avoiding details, but a lot of family disputes involve money, and we are not unique. In fact, I've been amazed by how many friends tell similar tales about their extended families when I mention the problems in mine. A lot of us are a mess. I miss my siblings, but I have no indication that they miss me. I know I cannot please them. I can't change the past, and I especially can't change their version of the past. I regret our rift. I pray for their health and happiness. Since family feuds between a few affect the many, I would love to renew our relationships, for them to know my grandchildren and I theirs, and for our children to be on speaking terms, but I don't think there's any corresponding interest in that outcome. I know that the current conventional wisdom counsels cutting the toxic people out of your life, and I am their toxicity.

I have had to make my peace with the silence.

But now two of my children are on the outs, and I am just so damn sad about it. Our last family gathering, for which I had high hopes of reconciliation, involved one shunning the other so obviously that everyone was uncomfortably aware of how A thought B was toxic. I don't know that we'll ever manage to host another gathering of the whole family, of all our kids. Maybe it will happen at my funeral? Or their father's? There's some happy thinking. My husband and I now visit our kids separately, which is geographically easy but hard on my heart. Our family is compartmentalized. Given my own failed history of sibling love, I feel incapable of guiding them to a resolution. I battle feelings of maternal failure with attempts at acceptance. I hide from the role of peacemaker because my deeper fear is that my quest to reconcile them will lead to one of them feeling chosen and one of them, lost to me. I'm devastated that the curse is to be my legacy.

My beloved children are adults. Two of them are nursing the hurt of some deep conflict of which I do not know the details. I know the feelings on both sides are valid and strong. I know not to take sides. I watched my own mother, who, before she died, fanned the flames of resentment among her children. She took the side of whomever she was with, and she actually enjoyed the drama that her revelation of confidential information provoked. For all my mother's qualities that I never wished to see in myself, this pitting of her children against each other is the biggest.

Yet my children are pitted against each other. Whatever I may have taught them about love was not enough.

We are done raising our children once they've become adults, but we never stop holding them in our hearts. We never stop rejoicing with their joy or sorrowing with their sorrow. These two kids of mine have so much in common, and I pray to God that they will rediscover their bond someday. I pray to God above that they will not spend their lives indifferent to each other, that their respective families will not be strangers to each other. I know from wretched experience, however, that blood is not as thick as I was once led to believe.

Walk through Zion, walk all around her; that you may tell the next generation that such is our God.

—Ps 48:12–14

CHAPTER 11

The Stuff We Leave

How could a thing remain unless you willed it; or be preserved
had it not been called forth by you?

—Wis 11:25

If you've had to clear out your parents' home after they've moved
or died or any other loved one's stuff, you are familiar with the
sinking thought of someone cleaning out your belongings. You
picture your kids wondering, "Why did my mom save all this
s—t?" and you shudder. We can make the inevitable process easier
with a little forethought, putting our affairs in order and paying
attention to establishing things like a will, an advanced health
directive, and burial/funeral wishes.

"What about this?" my youngest sister asked. She was elbow-deep
in a box of old VHS tapes in our parents' garage. With our dad's
death and our mother's move into assisted living, my siblings
and I were working against the clock on downsizing their long

life together. The house was in escrow, and we were sorting the remainder of our folks' unwanted stuff into manageable piles, heaps we'd defined as give away, sell, ditch, or keep. In the battered box, amid musicals featuring Fred Astaire and boxed sets of World War II documentaries, my sister had found a homemade cassette tape labeled only with our dad's name.

"Keep, I guess," I said, hoping it was not some deeply disillusioning discovery, a criminal court transcript, or a secret other family—you never know what might turn up in someone's belongings. "We'll figure it out later."

My sister traveled back home once our tasks were finished, and I forgot about the cassette tape. But she did not. She listened to it. Then she asked our mutual brother-in-law, who is a sound engineer, to transfer the recording to a CD, a copy of which he recently gave me. I am so glad we did not toss that tape into the ditch pile, because it contained a treasure beyond price: recordings of our dad's voice-over classes.

My dad had the kind of voice that commanded attention and filled a room. It was at once clear and deep, resonant yet relaxed. A consummate salesman, he'd made his fortune in the business world. All his adult life, however, people had told him that he should market his voice for radio or TV narration. Apparently, after he'd sold his finance company and was at loose ends, he'd taken a ten-week course to explore the possibility. He never pursued this second career, but the work he'd done for his classes was preserved on a cassette tape, which had ended up in a sagging cardboard box of outdated technology in the garage.

My dad was not a saver and nowhere near a hoarder. He got rid of books and magazines as soon as he'd read them, and he periodically weeded through his clothes. He used to pride himself on the empty space in his garage. He had no use for collections for the sake of collecting. Most of the things whose fate we'd debated were my mother's collectibles, along with household items that she no longer needed. But the stuff my dad had saved betrayed a sentimentality he did not often admit to, things like a grandchild's drawing or an old valentine or letters from his U.S. Navy days—or that cassette tape.

And though we have plentiful and wonderful photos of my dad, precious bits of silent home movies, and later, muffled videotapes of family events, we have little audio of his voice. I waited until the house was empty before I listened to the CD because I was certain I would cry. But I didn't: the voice-over classes were too delightful, too funny, and too exactly true. They flooded me with such intimacy of memory: my dad, reading advertising copy, taking direction before a redo, and best of all, summoning his own specific memories of joy or pride or surprise at the prompting of the instructor in order to tap into the reserve of honest emotions that the art of acting requires. The recordings present my dad as a student, a muser, a plumber of emotional depths, all delivered with the immediacy of his recorded voice, a voice that I surely couldn't forget but that had faded a little in my mind. I welcomed its familiar ring and cadence like a dear friend I hadn't heard from in years.

Condensing the large houseful of my parents' belongings into my mother's one-room apartment had put me on a warpath to declutter my own life. I'd begun to judge my belongings through the eyes of my children. I pictured them asking each other, "Why on earth did she save *this*?" I'd been going through my drawers and boxes and disposing of things with a critical ruthlessness. But that cassette tape, something my dad saved that he probably thought was silly, has given me pause in my quest to simplify. Maybe the fate of some things is best left to posterity to decide. As my dad's lark has become my treasure, a tangible reminder of how lovable he was, it occurs to me that maybe the legacy we leave is not ultimately up to us.

The truck is here, along with four can-do young men paid to lift and carry and deliver all the things we have packed. I can hardly count all the moves of our past, when my husband and I rented a truck and moved everything ourselves, from our parents moving into assisted living, to daughters moving from apartment to apartment, to us moving from city to town or from house to house, to friends moving and needing help. We are older now and a bit more solvent, hence the blessed young men.

Moving is an especially American option. We are a mobile society. We grow with shallow roots. We move for a better job, for more affordable housing, or just for the adventure. When I was in high school, my parents packed up six kids and left their extended families on the East Coast for a lucrative opportunity in Southern California. It felt as though we were moving to the moon. My husband grew up on various army bases, so he often had to move far from his comfort zone with little notice. We think that is why we refrained from moving our four kids while they were in school: because we both knew too well the exquisite torture of being the new kid.

But it's time. We are currently moving our now-empty nest from a community where we have lived for over thirty years to be close to my husband's possibly final job before retirement. It's only fifty miles away, but we are leaving behind a seriously established life.

There is so much stuff we have unearthed: years of classroom materials from my husband's teaching career, bins of yellowing newspaper and magazine clips from my writing career, boxes of memories stored by grown children moving to smaller digs, two storage containers of the Hummel figurines that my mother lovingly collected and that no one really wants now that she is gone, and three huge bags of baby clothes. Baby clothes! My baby is twenty-five. Why have I saved these things?

I gave the baby clothes to the local thrift store but not before shaking some of them out and remembering, *marveling over,* when my kids were tiny enough to wear them. A few of the outfits have been immortalized in photographs. I wanted to keep them; I foolishly felt like I was giving away a little part of myself with those clothes. I am still a mother, but I'm nothing like the mother who washed and folded those clothes. She is gone, and maybe some other mother will dress her little girl in a wee flowered sundress or embroidered French overalls that say, "Bébé."

I know from cataloging and dispersing my parent's possessions after they died that many of the things my husband and I insist on keeping will make no sense to our children when we are gone. We hold on to things for which we have no real use and which will have no meaning to anyone else—like those baby clothes. They were ridiculously hard for me to part with, and yet a lightened sense of freedom came from letting them go.

The moving men work together like a well-choreographed dance team, gliding through the house with dollies and strapping quilted blankets around our furniture. Looking at the stacks of boxes they are hauling outside to be trucked to our new home, I think of the many refugees around the world who must leave their homes with only the things they can carry—and maybe even with only the children they can carry—and I feel gluttonous. Will I wear all those shoes or cook with all those pots and pans or hang all those frames or, my particular downfall, ever read any of those books again? Why do we weigh ourselves down with all these things? Why do we think we need so much stuff? A monk's cell is suddenly attractive to me.

If life goes according to plan, and I know how naive that sounds, the move after this one will be our last. In five years or so, we aim to downsize drastically from the newly rented house, buy our retirement cottage somewhere, and live there till death do us part. It's a working plan, and I know that God and the universe could throw a lot of wrenches into it.

For now we sweep and mop the old house one last time, a bit embarrassed by our indifferent housekeeping: we witness the dust and gunk and dog hair revealed when large items are relocated. ("That's nothing," one of the nonjudgmental movers tells my husband. "Once we found an actual *mouse's nest* under a pillow on someone's bed.")

We clean and reminisce. We order a pizza. We take some ibuprofen for our aches. We think ahead to unpacking all those boxes. We will make the new place a home and try to remember to be grateful for each new day granted us.

If you're anything like me (and chances are that if you've picked up this book to read, you *are*), your nest has been emptied of your little birds for quite some time, and you've successfully applied for Medicare: Okay, boomer! You've done a lot in your life, and you still have good years ahead. You are involved in the lives of your children and grandchildren, and you'd do anything for them. Here's a way to show how much you really love your children: do the paperwork.

I mean the legal paperwork of a mature life: a will or a trust, a durable power of attorney, and an advanced health directive. You can go online or hire a lawyer, but you need to get these documents done. Then you have to let your designated executor know where you keep this important trove. When you're gone, your children will thank you.

I can be smug because my husband and I have recently completed the above-mentioned job. But I should hang my head in shame that we hadn't taken care of this long before. I guess you could say we played the odds of life and won. But what if we had both died while our kids were still minors? What would have happened to them? We were negligent parents, legally speaking. We had excuses: Who had the time back then? Who had the money? We often talked about being responsible parents, but in retrospect, we were not.

In the expected natural order, children outlive their parents. (Please, God!) We may have to care for our parents physically in their old age, and we bury them when they die. For Catholics, arranging the funeral of a parent is a holy task: our parents brought us into the Church through baptism, and we see them out on their way home to God. Having buried both of my parents, I know how helpful it is to know your parents' last wishes. This is to say that I know how unhelpful it is not to know what they want and not to have ever had the difficult but vital conversations about dying and death. In my case my mother outlived my father, but bless her heart, she abdicated her responsibility for his funeral with her philosophy of life being that if you never made a decision, you couldn't be blamed for things not working out well. So my siblings and I did what we thought was best. We chose the cemetery. We chose cremation. We chose the readings and the music for my dad's and, later, my mom's funeral Masses. We tried to honor our parents without really knowing if we were. It was unsettling.

My folks had established a family trust, but they had not put anything into the trust. We thought that they had signed advanced health directives, but we didn't know where they were or how to access them. When my father was gravely ill, my sister and I were certain that he did not want any extraordinary measures taken to prolong his life artificially. As we told the doctor this, my mother accused us of trying to kill off our dad. That was not a fun day.

After my dad died, I found the leather satchel with the paperwork establishing the trust and their advanced health directives. His last wishes were as we thought.

"Well," my mother said triumphantly, "at least you see that I want everything done to save me! Don't pull my plug!"

I showed her, with private amusement, where she had better make some legal updates, as the document she had signed years ago stipulated that nothing extraordinary be done on her behalf as well. Over the next seven years, my mother slowly succumbed to Parkinson's disease, but it happened on her own time, with all possible medical intervention. She never changed her directive legally, but thanks to that one outburst, we knew what she wanted, and we honored it.

When we parents put to paper our intentions for our health care and our wealth distribution, we can avoid any misunderstandings or machinations on the part of our heirs. No one likes to think about one's own death, but we can be sure that the event will not be prevented by our inattention. No one likes to think that in the absence of any instructions, our children will not be their best selves. But we've heard the stories. We know that money can bring out the worst of greed and selfishness in people. We all know the power of an inheritance to divide a family.

Once we are gone, we cannot control the narrative. The best we can do is leave a blueprint to be followed. That's why I think of these legal documents as a labor of love for our children. My aunt and uncle, God rest them, had planned for everything surrounding their deaths, from prepaid burial arrangements to the musical requests for their funerals. My cousins were able to grieve secure in the knowledge that they were carrying out their parents' wishes. The hymns my aunt and uncle had chosen were endearing guitar-Mass throwbacks to the seventies, which indicated to me that they had stipulated these instructions long before they died. But seeing the serenity on my cousins' tear-streaked faces made me realize that I owe my children the same active, helpful love that my aunt and uncle had modeled for me.

Talking about death is a social taboo. I am always amazed by the number of people I know who have never been to a funeral and who have never discussed death with their loved ones. We can hide from it and sanitize it and ignore it, but our death will have to be dealt with by somebody. With a bit of forethought, we can love our children one last time from the grave. Where there's literally a will, there's a way.

The funeral discussion with an elderly parent is a tough one. As mentioned, when my dad died, my mother went along with the decisions her kids made regarding his burial. Seven years later, my mother was also cremated. Their ashes are buried together in the plot they now share in the cemetery under an old oak tree.

But I well remember the times I'd tried to bring the topic up with both of them. "Well, that's morbid, and I don't want to think about it," my mother would say. And that would be the end of it. Having learned that lesson, I've let my kids know my final wishes.

Except that now I think my final wishes are changing.

I thought I wanted to be cremated, which was mainly to spare the expense of the fancy casket that funeral home workers sometime guilt-trip survivors into purchasing as a sign of love for the departed. I mean, it's all just going underground. As a Catholic, I know that my remains, whether ashes or a preserved body in a coffin, must be buried rather than scattered or kept in an urn on the mantel. I don't have a preference as to the location of the cemetery—I suppose somewhere any of my kids might want to visit. They know I want a funeral Mass. They know the priest I'd like to say the Mass, assuming he outlives me. It all seemed like a done deal.

Until I learned about green burials.

Specifically, a company in Seattle has changed my mind. The company, called Recompose, is a licensed green funeral home in Washington State. While a green burial simply means that the unembalmed body is placed directly into the earth to decompose, Recompose goes beyond this practice. Their process, called natural organic reduction (NOR), or human composting, became legal in Washington in 2019. It is now permissible in Oregon, where I live. Legislation is pending in several other states.

I know, human composting sounds horrifying, like something Charlton Heston would have discovered in the movie

Soylent Green, a 1973 movie that is coincidentally set in the dystopian future year of 2022. But the company's description of their new development in the treatment of earthly remains is reassuring, at least to me. To quote from Recompose's website (www.recompose.life), "Your loved one's body will be surrounded by wood chips, alfalfa, and straw in a vessel where microbes will naturally break the body down. The entire process, from placing your person into the vessel to finished soil, takes between six to eight weeks." The resulting soil, like the ashes of a loved one after cremation, can then be claimed and similarly spread or buried. Or the company will donate the soil to a nonprofit land trust area in Washington if the family prefers not to keep the remains: one cubic yard of soil is a lot of soil.

There are many reasons this method appeals to me, the first of which is the fact that my grandchildren deserve an inhabitable planet. Of the 3 million people who die in the United States each year, about 1.6 million people are cremated, a process that requires fossil fuels heated to high temperatures and that releases carbon dioxide and other particulates into the atmosphere. In human composting, the carbon matter contained in each body is returned to the earth. For every person choosing human composting over cremation, one metric ton of carbon dioxide does not enter the atmosphere. I like the idea that after death, I can leave behind choices, however small, that are environmentally friendly and will reduce my carbon footprint.

I previously decided to opt for cremation because it is cheaper than a conventional burial, and I am cheap. I note that the cost of human composting is similar to cremation. The ceremony, flowers, and newspaper obituaries are extra, but that is true of most funerals, at least the ones I've had a hand in planning.

My one reason not to choose this type of burial is that my religion does not yet approve of this particular technology. The Church did not permit cremation for dead bodies until 1963, but I hope that, given the demonstrable good that human composting does for the earth and for the living, it will be deemed allowable by the time I go. If not, my conscience may have to prevail.

Now I just have to decide if I should "precompose" and lock in today's rate. Like I said, it's a tough conversation. But it is one well worth having before you go.

Sometimes when I watch my daughter mothering her daughter, I feel the eyes of history in me and around me. I am so entranced by watching my daughter change a diaper or chase her little one around the couch or comfort her baby after a scare, and I suddenly see my mother watching me mother this child of mine thirty-odd years ago, as well as her mother watching her mother me sixty-odd years ago, and so on and so on—the line of mothers and daughters visible like a long, fine fishing wire, the beginning of which is centuries away.

Each new generation of mothers does the job differently. We grandmothers want to be helpful and pass on the wisdom of our parenting, but much of what we have to offer is obsolete. My mother's ways were old-fashioned to me, and now my ways are antiquated to my daughter. I get that, I really do—but still. Maybe all we can pass on is the fierceness of our love, the intensity of our commitment to mothering. I think of Ukrainian grandmas and Afghani grandmas and Israeli grandmas and Palestinian grandmas amid the daily news of wars abroad. I ask God to bless and keep them as they give all their strength and all they have to protect their children and grandchildren. Mothers and daughters are carrying on their work in far more dangerous circumstances than my own.

Awash in joy at the sight of my daughter delighting in my granddaughter figuring out how to jump, I feel the older eyes of our foremothers around us, just as my heart feels the tug of the memory of all the little girls turning into mothers. I imagine my mother felt the same when watching me embark on the adventure of motherhood, but she didn't really say, and I didn't notice. Becoming a grandmother has given me insight into the deep well of wonder my mother must have felt when she became a grandmother. New mothers are wrapped up in new babies and don't have a lot of patience for anything else. At least I didn't. I tuck away my regret for all the times I was blind to the eyes that loved me.

A child or a city will preserve one's name, but better than either, finding wisdom.

—Sir 40:19

CHAPTER 12

The Afterlife

For who knows God's counsel, or who can conceive what the
Lord intends?

—Wis 9:13

A few days before my dad died, I heard him singing softly to
himself: "Show me the way to go home / I'm tired and I wanna
go to bed." I remembered the song from when I was a kid, and my
mind filled in the next lyrics.

He sang those two lines a bunch of times in a row, possibly
all the words he could remember. He was a little bit hallucinatory
as his oxygen levels dropped and his heart continued to falter. I
knew he was ready to go home. He'd made sure my mother had a
safe place to live, his affairs were pretty much in order, and he was
just waiting to be shown the way home.

So he was singing—and talking. I didn't realize until later that
he maybe was praying, that he was asking God to guide him on
his way home.

My mom, my siblings, and the grandkids spent time just
sitting with my dad after the hospice nurses told us that his
remaining time was short. Family members were arriving by the

hour. Something told me to write down everything my dad said the day before he died, before the morphine took over and he was never really conscious again.

"It's incredible. It's unbelievable!" he said.

Then he said, "They're all around me." He said this several times, looking toward the window each time he said this, gazing into the distance, distracted, surprised, and smiling. His body kept jolting as though something was repeatedly waking him up. After one jolt he said confidentially, looking me square in the eyes, "It's scaring the crap out of me!" Before I could respond, his attention reverted back to whatever miracle in the clouds he was witnessing.

A lot of what he said was unintelligible, and we asked him to speak more loudly. At one point he seemed to say, "Where's the beef?" I repeated the question and asked him if that's what he'd said, and he said, "Yeah!"

Where's the beef? Was he asking God?

We took turns talking to him, mentioning the new house that he had just moved into ("Whose house is this?" he asked my sister at one point), our plans for the Fourth of July, whatever we thought he might like to hear. We reassured him that everything was fine, that our mom was situated and taken care of, that he had no worries. He seemed restless but was unable to get out of bed.

"You're doing fine," I said to him.

"What am I doing?" he asked incredulously.

"You're doing whatever you need to do," I said, feeling inadequate.

"Hmmph," he said. He died on the Fourth of July.

I've since learned that dying people often experience what is called end-of-life dreams and visions (ELDVs) and that nurses and hospice workers have come to realize that when a hospice patient reports seeing deceased loved ones, the end is nigh. According to Dr. Christopher Kerr's research, as is told in his TEDx Talk and in his book, *Death Is but a Dream*, these ELDVs can help the dying make sense of their dying. I'm pretty sure the beings who were "all around" my dad were his deceased family members—because he saw them. It may have scared the crap out of him because, in our past conversations when he was lucid, he hadn't been so sure about God. Now he had a sense that he was being welcomed home, and I imagine he hadn't expected that.

I grieved hard for my beloved dad. I prayed that he found the beef and that the incredible, unbelievable folks all around him took him by the hand and led him home. Later I thought of the last lines of that old drinking song: "Wherever I may roam / On land or sea or foam / You will always hear me singing this song / Show me the way to go home." All these years later, I still hear my dad, the old sailor, singing this song; it plays on even now, after all his roaming and now that he's been shown the way home.

The stories of the dying having such powerful visions made me remember something about my mother's last days. Over the course of the seven years after my father died, my mom, who had long suffered from Parkinson's and related dementia, lived with my sister, then moved from independent living to assisted living in the same facility, and finally, to a small twenty-four-hour-care home. She was angry with us about the last move and gave us the silent treatment. The man in charge of the home told us not to worry, that such moves were hard on people in her condition, and that she'd come around. He mentioned that she'd really relaxed after someone from the local church brought her Holy Communion.

I wondered then about who exactly had brought her Communion. I'd brought my mom to Mass at that parish many times after my dad died, when she was still somewhat mobile, and she always fixated on an older gentleman in another pew close to the altar who really did resemble my dad, at least in profile. My mom would stare at him quite obviously throughout Mass. She would smile at him flirtatiously. Once she tried to follow him out to the parking lot, but he'd left early: he was one of the Eucharistic ministers who brought Communion to the homebound. It all of a sudden clicked for me. What if that guy had brought her Communion? My mom may have thought my dad had come to her room, that he'd come back from the dead for her. He was her vision, but he was real flesh and blood. Not only had she relaxed after that mysterious visit, she stopped eating and died shortly thereafter. I never investigated whether that man had been the one to minister to my mom. But I liked to imagine her face at the sight of my dad's doppelgänger walking into her room. It made me happy to picture her happy.

When you lose someone you love so freaking much, you just can't believe that nothing remains of them, that, as the old saying goes, that's all she wrote. At least I can't. Their body may be dead, but what about their spirit? Their essence? Their soul? I can't buy it. I sometimes sense the presence of those I've lost, and I know I am not alone in this experience. The Irish speak of the "thin places," where the membrane between earth and heaven is transparent, where space and time are suspended, and where the spiritual kisses the physical. I am certain I have found myself there.

But I can't prove the existence of the afterlife. I can't prove heaven. I can't prove God. Even the riveting stories of near-death experiences and end-of-life visions can be explained by physiological factors. The thing about faith is that you have to come to an understanding, however uneasy, with mystery. You have to be okay with knowing you can't know, with not knowing anything for sure. You have to get comfortable with the fact that your little mind cannot know God's mind. When you make your peace with the unknowable, you inhabit faith.

Heaven has been presented to me in many ways. When I was a child, I accepted that dead people turned into angels and lived high above us in the heavens. They wore white gowns—even the men—and a halo glowed just above their hair. They played little harps and were happy for eternity. I'd seen paintings. It all made sense. Then I got a little earth science in school, and the logistics of another world in the clouds seemed problematic. Wouldn't the space capsules have to pass through it on the way to the moon? Maybe heaven was farther up than the moon, maybe even past Pluto. Also, wouldn't playing the little harp all day get boring? Oh, but there was no time in heaven. No calendar. This additional information made heaven sound terminally boring. Maybe the dead people got to watch the live people living their lives. Anything was better than the other place, where the bad people go: H-E-double-hockey-sticks (L-L), where the devil cranked up the heat until your whole body (body? soul?) was on fire and you screamed in agony all day. Except there was no time down there either. Hell was deep under the ground, possibly in the center of the earth, although everyone knew that all the digging would get you to China sooner than to hell, which was another conundrum for science to explain.

When my grandmother died, I learned that heaven was like a celestial family reunion, and my grandma would be reunited with the grandfather I'd never met, as well as all her siblings, her parents, their parents, and so on. It was a sad time for those of us left on earth without her but a happy time for her. How old would she be in heaven? Would her husband who died young recognize her? How would her second husband fit into the picture? I was told I was being too practical, if not too impertinent. Her body was the first dead body I'd ever seen. She looked hollow, like a mummy, but was cold and hard to the touch. Death seemed much more real than heaven.

By the time I was in high school, I'd learned the word agnostic, which was a more sophisticated way of saying I was over the Catholicism of my childhood. This was the era of civil rights and feminism, when everything was shifting and changing, and I saw only racists and hypocrites among the adults in church. Then I gravitated to atheist, which made so much sense to a worldly teenager like myself. I totally got that whole riff that religion was the opiate of the masses—thank you, Karl Marx—and that man was the only creature who knew he was going to die, so he invented God to keep from going mad from the knowledge. When I enrolled at a Catholic university and was told I'd be required to take three semesters of theology, I understood suffering because I was going to have to suffer through these classes for my degree. The registrar would not allow me to uncheck the box that said "Catholic" on my application. Since I'd won a partial scholarship and I got to live away from home, which had been my main goal, I figured I'd tough it out. I'd ask those professors all my doubts in the form of smart-ass questions, and they'd be stumped.

Except they weren't. They were thoughtful and flexible. They were open to discussion. They were wise but humble. They educated me in a way that God and God's love began to make some kind of sense to my heart of stone. Somehow, they gave me back the faith of my childhood in adult language. I think a lot of it had to do with the fact that they were comfortable with mystery. Mystery was their ever-present companion on the journey. They taught me that the journey matters and that heaven is another word for home.

St. Paul tells us that at the moment of death, at our final judgment, we will say our yes or our no to God, and that will determine our eternal fate. We can choose God, or we can choose not-God. If heaven is coming home to the presence of God, then hell is God's absence. Who would choose that? Who would reject God? It seems possible that heaven is in everyone's future—even Caligula's or Hitler's or Idi Amin's. We assume that only God gets to ask the question and only God gets to judge. In the afterlife everything is possible, and nothing is impossible. This scenario does not satisfy my own personal thirst for justice, my own taste for schadenfreude. But it does jibe with God's penchant for mercy.

I believe in an afterlife of which I have no actual concept because I believe in an actual, if ineffable, God. And I believe in God because I have sensed God, I have relied on God. I have seen God in so many places, in so many hearts, and in so many small slices of life. I have heard too much from God to think I've perhaps only imagined God. I'm not that creative.

"Do not be afraid," says the Lord in Revelation (1:17–18), "I hold the keys to death and the netherworld." But we are naturally afraid of the unknown. Death is our greatest unknown. It's scary. It's also inevitable, at least for our corporal bodies. Even as we sense them falling apart on us, our will to live rages on. Even with a strong faith in the afterlife, we can be surprised by the grip with which we cling to this life.

Sometimes this life seems easy and natural: I wake up and thank the Lord above for another day. It's simple. Other times existence seems extraordinarily weird, and we wonder, How is any of this happening? Any theory seems plausible: We are all some kid's eighth-grade science project. We are each a reincarnated soul. We are only one version of the multiverse. We are in a simulation. We are in the Matrix. We are collectively dreaming. In other words, we aren't who we think we are. We aren't even real.

Our human gift is to speculate on what we don't know, to imagine solutions to riddles, and to crave order. Our human anxiety grows with the fact that we can't know. Faith is salted with doubt. Faith will drive your mind crazy before it settles in your core.

As I age, I know more and more people who are dead. Every anniversary, my husband and I pull out our wedding photos, and lately, we feel a bit mortal as we note the many wedding guests from over forty years ago who have since died. My paternal grandmother had the morbid habit of drawing a stark X through people's faces in her photo albums when they died. We aren't there yet.

But on All Souls' Day, I feel the spirits of my beloved dead all around me. Every year, I make an altar for them, not a beautiful *ofrenda* like some of my friends erect, with favorite refreshments and painted skulls and strings of marigolds, but just a little table with candles lighting the holy cards and handouts from the funerals I've attended. I prop up their smiling faces. I'm happy to see them. I pray with them. I sit with them: my dad, my mom, and my niece, as well as my grandparents and aunts and uncles and cousins and friends who have gone forth from us. Some of them died at a ripe old age. But some deaths have felt like utter devastation—those loved ones who died too soon, too young, too tragically, and too incomprehensibly.

My heart holds great lumps of grief for them. Some days it overflows with raw spillage. Having said that, having felt that, I do believe my beloved dead are at peace. I sense their peace. All Souls' Day, or el Día de los Muertos, reminds us that life does not end with our corporeal demise but rather changes into something eternal and holy and full of grace and mercy: the communion of saints.

The Bible presents us with many images and promises of the afterlife, for the moment we will dwell with our loving God. I can't imagine what that could be, what that could look like or feel like. None of us can. I'm just grateful that someday I will know, even as my photo may be added to someone else's little table: a joyful soul among all joyful souls.

The more people I lose, the more people I mourn, the more I feel in my guts that they are not gone. Even as I grieve a loved one's death, I believe in their life after life. I sense the change in their existence. As I get closer to that change myself, I see the holy in everything around me. I see glimmers of the answers we seek. I embrace the present, but I also walk with the waiting. Eventually, every warrior lays down their weapons and goes with God in sacred surrender.

�֍

God is a saving God for us; the Lord, my Lord, controls the passageways of death.

—Ps 68:21

Afterword

This is the fourth book I've written, and I've honestly thought that every book is my last. It's not that I think I'm going to die but that maybe I've got nothing left to say. I feel wrung out, like there's not a drop of anything new left in me. And when you're an old person writing about aging, the fact is that you really may have written your last book.

As that old person, though, I get that life is both cyclical and fantastically unpredictable. Life is a series of roundabouts. Life is full of surprises you should have expected but never saw coming. Life is hope and disappointment, love and regret, gratitude and longing, faith and backward steps. Life is a gift from God that we have to give back. But before my day comes, I may yet have a few things to feel, to know, and to write. Who can know the mind of God? Not any of us blessed, beloved mortals. We can only trust that God is with us always, "till the moon be no more" (Ps 72:7).

About the Author

Valerie Schultz is a freelance writer, journalist, and columnist for *The Bakersfield Californian*, as well as a contributing writer for the Jesuit publication *America* and the daily prayer book *Give Us This Day*. Her essays and short stories have appeared in the *Los Angeles Times*, the *Washington Post*, and the *Chicago Tribune*, as well as in Catholic publications such as *US Catholic*, *Commonweal*, *Human Development*, and the *National Catholic Reporter*. Her first book, *Closer: Essays on Marriage and Intimacy*, was published in 2008. Her award-winning book *Overdue: A Dewey Decimal System of Grace* is based on her work in a state prison library. Her latest book of essays, *A Hill of Beans: The Grace of Everyday Troubles*, was published in 2022. She lives on the Oregon Coast.